Black Money

*Created Through Smuggling and Counterfeiting
to Fund Terrorism*

Black Money

Created Through Smuggling and Counterfeiting to Fund Terrorism

Brij Bhardwaj

HAR-ANAND
PUBLICATIONS PVT LTD

HAR-ANAND PUBLICATIONS PVT LTD
E-49/3, Okhla Industrial Area, Phase-II, New Delhi-110020
Tel.: 41603490 Fax: 011-41708607
E-mail: info@haranandpublications.com/haranand@rediffmail.com
Website: www.haranandpublications.com

Copyright © Brij Bhardwaj, 2013

First Published: 2013

All rights reserved. No part of this publication may be reproduced, stored in a retrival system, or transmitted in any form or by any means, electronic, mechanical photocopying, recording or otherwise, without the prior written permission of the publishers.

Published by Ashok Gosain and Ashish Gosain for
Har-Anand Publications Pvt Ltd

Introduction

As the clamour for bringing black money stacked abroad in tax havens like Switzerland and other countries in Europe grows the country is looking to the Government of India for action. It is generally believed that the sums involved are huge and can go a long way in solving the problems of the country. The international opinion has also turned against countries which allowed their banks to accept deposits without verifying the antecedents and hid their tracks under the cover of secrecy of banking law. Pressure has grown in the wake of terrorist activities including the attack on U.S. to check flow of funds for criminal activities.

The result has been that many countries in Europe including Switzerland have started sharing information about funds kept by foreign nationals in their respective countries to enable the host countries to investigate if the funds in question were part of ill-gotten gains kept abroad to avoid detection. The Government has been working to investigate the details of the accounts received by them from different governments and agencies. In many cases the owners of such accounts have accepted the liability of withholding taxes and paid up while some more cases are under investigation.

It is no secret that businessmen, politicians, film stars and others are guilty of this practice and it is also known that flow of funds in reverse direction takes place during the elections. Much of it is part of money laundered which is estimated to be around two trillion dollars every year. According to United Nations office, Drugs and Crime, generate about three per cent of World GDP. The general myth that money launderer is an individual who has received huge sums of money as bribe and is keeping it abroad to conceal the same is not true.

The fact actually is that black money is generated by lakhs of individuals by evading payment of taxes. This includes not only tax on income but other taxes also like the excise and custom duties. Counterfeiting, smuggling is a major contributor in generating black money. All individuals who evade taxes are guilty of generating black money. So far there has been stress on finding out black money kept abroad or invested in land estates or in gold instead of looking at modus operandi of avoiding payment of taxes.

This according to experts amounts to shooting the messenger as what needs to be checked is the creation of a system which leads to the generation of black money. It is not an isolated effort or one time action but a continuous process which needs to be reversed. One can appreciate actions like getting information from foreign Governments about the money kept there and also collecting more intelligence by setting up more offices abroad. One can also follow up on suggestions made by different panels to check this through making laws more stringent, fast trial courts, and establishment of institutions like Lok Pal at Center and Lok Yukta in States.

But the basic problem which is crying for attention is widespread counterfeiting and smuggling which is leading to generation of black money on a huge scale not only in India, but world over. For instance counterfeiting is considered as world's fastest growing industry and current estimates show 10 per cent of world trade falls in this category. A recent study conducted by Business Action to stop counterfeiting and pirated goods currently estimated it at 600 to 650 billion US dollars which is likely to double by 2015.

The challenge posed by Counterfeiting and Smuggling has become the biggest challenge for Indian industry and the

Government because of loss of revenue and brand erosion. Action, however, is slow and sluggish because of low priority given to economic offences by the enforcement agencies including police whose pre-occupation with more serious crimes and law and order leaves little time for them to deal with white collar crimes. In some cases, for shortage of manpower or lack of knowledge and skills to tackle such crimes, they remain undetected.

According to a FICCI study spurious goods are available in pharmaceutical drugs, computer and software goods, soft drinks, cosmetics, toiletries and is also rampant in automobile goods. It is estimated that twenty per cent of total road accidents can be attributed directly or indirectly to counterfeit automobile parts whose values is estimated to be around Rs 2,500 crores. Estimates of fake or counterfeit medicines vary from five to twenty per cent. If counterfeiting and smuggling are checked thousands of additional jobs can be created.

Cigarettes smuggling has become a major security concern for many countries as many outfits like Al-Qaida and Taliban are turning to illicit trade to finance their activities. According to U.S Department of Justice Bureau Alcohol, Firearms and Tobacco are some of the items which are used to finance the activities of terrorists. These items being highly taxed offer big opportunity to smugglers and counterfeiters to make quick money as they are no longer interested in smuggling of gold or other luxury items.

A time has come when the political parties should divert their attention from only looking at avenues where black money is invested or kept and start plugging loopholes which help in its generation.

Role of Black Money and Accounts Held in Tax Havens

How widespread is smuggling of items across the borders from countries like Bangladesh, Nepal, Burma and Sri Lanka with which India has free trade agreements can be judged from the fact that goods worth Rs 71.5 crores were seized on Indo-Bangladesh border during the year 2011-2012, according to a Home Ministry sources. In reply to a question in Rajya Sabha it was stated that 24 persons were arrested in this connection. The smuggled items included fake Indian currency, ready-made garments, cigarettes, medicines and drugs. One has to accept that the quantity of seized goods is around ten per cent of what is smuggled across. One can easily add to this figure smuggling which takes place along other borders with Nepal, Mayanar, Sri Lanka and China.

With greater availability of imported goods including international brands, reduction of import duties traditional items like gold are not on top of the list for smuggling instead attention has shifted to items which attract high taxes in the country. In this connection cigarettes and liquor top the list. The craze for foreign cigarettes is also making it a top item on list for smugglers. Not only illegally manufactured cigarettes are more harmful for consumers but they also do not carry statutory warnings that they are harmful to health.

In Pakistan a major manufacturer Philip Moris has decided to stop production thus depriving the Pakistan Government of billions of rupees as revenue, as they found it impossible to compete with illegal manufacturers in price and with cigarettes smuggled into the country. This will hurt Pakistan economy According to estimate sale of smuggled cigarettes increased by sixty five per cent while sale of illegal ones rose by 15 per cent.

They come here from China, Mayamar, Nepal, Bangladesh, Indonesia and Pakistan. In a rare case a container load was caught in Agra indicating how widespread the problem is.

Any talk in India about black money is mainly focused on accounts held by Indian politicians and businessmen in tax havens based in different parts of the world particularly Switzerland, off shore banking hubs like Isle of Mann, and other such hubs in Europe, Latin America and Asia. It is no secret that a large number of Indians operate accounts overseas. These include businessmen who have earned commissions in defence deals, and those who have made money by under invoicing exports and over-invoicing imports. There are also politicians who park money earned by them while in office as bribes and commission in Government deals with foreign companies. Part of these funds come back to India during election time to finance poll campaigns.

There are various estimates about the money held abroad, the latest being made by the CBI chief. The figure is in trillions, but the general view is that the black money in circulation within the country is much more. Looking at the way in which real estate market operates in India, the large scale counterfeiting operations, smuggling and the corruption at different levels, all help in creation of black money. The Mafia operations, crime syndicates, clearly indicate that a large part of our economy is outside the tax net and operates freely in the current climate.

The new taxation policy which has lowered the tax limit and various amnesty schemes have not been able to make a dent as it continues to be easy to avoid paying taxes totally instead of operating legally. In any market in India one can see the working of parallel economy functioning in terms of counterfeit goods and smuggled goods which are sold freely not only in rural and remote areas but in all our big cities where the major operators are based. The size of this market is huge.

The latest estimates indicate that India is becoming a major destination for smuggling and Counterfeiting in the world for branded goods. Items like Cigarettes, liquor, textiles, electronic items, mobiles are some of the major items on the list of smuggling while counterfeiting covers all major industries operating in India. Counterfeiting is being done not only in the country but also in some countries as a part of State policy. The flow of such goods into India from countries around us has become easy after India signed free trade agreements with these countries.

In some cases container loads of smuggled goods have been seized indicating a strong spurt in such activity. Every vendor in cities keeps a stock of smuggled cigarettes, electronic goods and mobiles. While rural markets are flooded with counterfeit merchandise for daily use by consumers. They include items of daily use like toothpaste, soaps, creams and items like spare parts for automobiles, ink cassettes for printing and spurious drugs which endanger lives. There is hardly an item which is not being marketed by units engaged in manufacture of counterfeit.

Let me give some estimates about the extent of such operations.

Brij Bhardwaj

Contents

1. Fighting Counterfeit with Global Standards — 13
2. Challenges Facing the Indian Manufacturing Industry — 31
3. Enforcement of Anti-Counterfeit and Anti-Smuggling Laws — 35
4. Curbing Counterfeiting Through Taxation — 42
5. Industries Affected by Counterfeiting — 47
6. Counterfeiting and Piracy Pose Danger for Consumers — 58
7. Public Awareness—Sword against Counterfeiting and Smuggling — 64
8. Contraband Cigarettes Big Business — 71
9. Introduction to Counterfeiting and its Impact on Automotive Sector — 74
10. Conclusion — 130
    Counterfeit and Smuggling: Research Report Findings — 132
    Annexures — 134
    Index — 175

Chapter 1

Fighting Counterfeit with Global Standards

About GS1 India

GS1 India is a not for profit standards body set up by the Ministry of Commerce, Govt. of India and leading Chambers of Commerce comprising CII, FICCI, ASSOCHEM, IMC, FEIO besides BIS, IIP, Spices Board and APEDA to educate and assist Indian Industry in Adoption of global standards used in supply chain management for facilitating faster movement of physical goods and related information flow electronically. It is affiliated to GS1, Brussels which oversees a network of over 110 GS1 organisations worldwide.

The magnitude and effects of counterfeiting is of such significance that it compels strong and sustained action from governments, business and consumers. More effective enforcement is critical in this regard, as is the need to build public support to combat counterfeiting. Increased co-operation between governments and industry would be beneficial, as would better data collection to address safety and security issues of the supply chains.

Based on growing threat of counterfeits, many countries have started addressing vulnerabilities in the supply chain by enacting legislation, vigilance and surveillance against counterfeit products entering the legitimate supply chain which requires to be complemented through global standards for unique identification, capture and share information supporting supply chain visibility.

This chapter is intended as a motivator for change and a foundation for stakeholder dialogue. It explains how global standards can assist in fight against counterfeit and illicit trade by:

- Providing a commonsense definition of visibility that can easily be applied to multiple industries and business processes;
- Describing the standards, processes and technologies that can uniquely identify objects and activities to provide visibility throughout organizations and supply chains;
- Presenting examples of how organizations in various industries have used these standards and technologies to manage inventory, prevent diversion, ensure product authenticity and safety, facilitate recalls, meet documentation and reporting requirements, track and manage assets, and improve other business processes;
- Documenting how standards-based approaches enable more productive and mutually beneficial relationships among trading partners.
- Describing an interoperable framework for authentication and verification services.

By understanding the common elements needed for brand protection, along with the standards and infrastructure services that support them, organisations and governments can make informed decisions on the options available to reduce both business and consumer risk.

Industry Challenges

Counterfeiting has grown from localised operations into highly profitable global businesses with mass production, global sales and distribution networks. Counterfeit physical objects[1] can be found

---

[1] In physical objects, in this paper, physical objects are intended to mean all physical objects, including raw materials, components, sub-assemblies, finished products, assets such as pallets and containers. For simplicity, the terms physical objects, products and goods will be used interchangeably.

in almost every country and in virtually all sectors of the global economy. Counterfeits are often substandard and can pose serious health and safety risks, with an estimated 3,000 deaths annually in the G20 member countries. The World Health Organization reports that 700,000 die annually from counterfeit prescription drugs.

In 2011, the Paris-based Business Alliance to Stop Counterfeit and Piracy (BASCAP) estimated that the counterfeit and piracy market is growing annually at 22%. Its size could reach USD $1.77 trillion by 2015.

Figure 1: The Complete Picture (referenced BASCAP report)

OECD Category	Estimate in $ billions (2008)	Estimate in $ billions (2015)
Internationally traded counterfeit and pirated products	$285 - $360	$770 - $960
Domestically produced and consumed counterfeit and pirated products	$140 - $215	$370 - $570
Digitally pirated products	$30 - $75	$80 - $240
Sub total	**$455 - $650**	**$1,220 - $1,770**
Broader economy wide effects+	$125	$125 +
Employment losses*	2.5 million	2.5 million +

Source: *Frontier Economics.*

Organised criminal[3] groups are seen as playing an increasing role in counterfeiting. They are benefitting from highly profitable operations, perceived as low risk in terms of apprehension and prosecution. Counterfeiters undermine and compete with legitimate business. The impact on intellectual property rights

---

[2]*Estimating the global economic and social impacts of counterfeiting and piracy.* Business Alliance to Stop Counterfeit and Piracy, February 2011.

[3]*Trafficking in illicit goods.* http://www.interpol.int/Crime-areasffrafficking-in-illicit-goodsffrafficking-in-illicit-goods. *Trafficking in illicit goods.* http://www . internol. int/Crime-areas/Trafficking- in-illicit -goods/Trafficking- in-illicit-goods. Interpol, 2012.

(IPR) holders can be significant across core aspects of their business and results in an estimated 2.5 million lost in the G20 countries.

Counterfeiting harms national interests including public safety and national security. Governments are deprived of revenues and taxes and under constant pressure for allocation of scarce resources to market surveillance and counter-measures to combat illicit trade activities. G20 member countries lose an estimated US $77.5 billion in tax revenues, have higher welfare spending due to lost jobs, and incur US $25 billion in increased costs to fight crime due to counterfeiting.[4]

Continued growth in the online sale of pirated and counterfeit hard goods will soon surpass the volume of such goods sold by street vendors and in other physical markets.[5]

Trends in Counterfeiting and Deceptive Practices

The counterfeit market has primary and secondary victims. The primary victims are the consumers, corporate buyers and small businesses who believe what they have bought to be authentic and safe. The secondary victims buy knowingly and do not know they need protection from toxic, unsafe and dangerous counterfeits. Strategies and counter measures to combat these sub-markets will differ. Counterfeiters will use every means possible to deceive authorities and their primary market customers.

Trends

- Increasing use of the Internet as a sales channel for counterfeit physical objects resulting in a warning from experts that Internet sales of counterfeit products will soon overtake offline sales.

[4]*Estimating the global economic and social impacts of counterfeiting and piracy.* Business Alliance to Stop Counterfeit and Piracy, February 2011.
[5]*2012 Special 301 Report.* www.ustr.gov/sites/default/files/2012%20Special%20301%20Report_O.pdf. U.S. Government, 2012.

- Increasing use of legitimate courier and regular post for small packages, is making it more difficult for enforcement to curtail such activity.

Deceptive practices
- Unbranded physical objects are shipped separately from their labels, insignia and brand packaging.
- Counterfeiters specialising in producing counterfeit labels, insignia or consumer packaging export these products to assemblers who complete the final assembly of the counterfeit objects.
- Counterfeit components or sub-assemblies are shipped separately to Free Trade Zones (FTZ) to be assembled and distributed within the FTZ or to countries outside the FTZ.
- FTZs are used to mask the origin of counterfeits.
- Part of a genuine shipment or container/pallet of goods are replaced with counterfeits (i.e. genuine and counterfeits co-mingled).
- Sales on the Internet of counterfeit goods indicated as excess, over-stock or returns.
- Consumer-to-consumer (C2C) sales of counterfeit products take place both online and offline.
- Differences and gaps in local laws, regulations and enforcement ability are taken advantage of to keep as many stages of counterfeit activities from being shut down for as long as possible, exposing lower-level traffickers to legal ramifications.
- Counterfeiters are no longer limited to consumer goods markets and increasingly target industrial sectors, including: agriculture, aerospace, automotive, rail, military and defence with counterfeit raw materials, components, tooling and supplies.

Figure 2: Views on trends and developments in counterfeiting and piracy, by economy DECD (2005b).

Economy	Expansion from luxury to common consumer goods	Increase in volumes of infringing goods	Increase in goods that represent a threat to public health and security	Growth of illegal activity on the internet	Organised crime is a factor
Australia	*	*	*	*	
Canada	*	*	*	*	*
France	*	*	*	*	*
Germany	*	*	*		
Hungary	*	*		*	*
Israel					
Japan		*		*	
Korea		*			
Mexico					
Netherlands		*	*		
New Zealand	*	*		*	
Poland	*			*	*
Portugal	*	*			*
Russia	*	*	*		*
Spain	*	*			
Sweden	*	*	*		
Switzerland		*		*	
Chinese Taipei	*			*	
European Union	*	*	*		*

There is no single method to guarantee the identity and authenticity of physical object across industries.

Mass serialization coupled with added security deterrents is a requirement in certain industry sectors as well as chain of custody or Pedigree (also called ePedigree). But these are components of a much wider brand protection strategy and not the end solution. Brand protection needs a multi-faceted approach to ensure:
- full chain Visibility
- full chain Traceability—the ability to trace back and track forward a product at any point of the supply chain
- consistent Data synchronization
- confidence in ability to be specific to a lot/batch in a recall situation (due to counterfeit)

- Integrity of Transportation and Logistics (T&L) systems.

Consideration should be given to managing the entire life cycle of an object from early design consideration to new product introduction, life cycle management to end of life planning. Embedding "design for traceablility" at the design concept stage of an object could help to reduce costs over the entire life cycle and could be instrumental in reducing the risk of counterfeits (Ref: Architecture view of safe and secure supply chain).

Figure 3: Architecture view of safe and secure supply chain

```
                    ┌─────────────────┐
                    │ Safe and Secure │
   Is the Object    │  Supply Chain   │   Is the chain of
     genuine?       └─────────────────┘   custody intact?
              ┌────────────┴────────────┐
      ┌───────────────┐         ┌───────────────┐
      │ Authentication│         │   Pedigree    │
      └───────────────┘         └───────────────┘
       ┌─────┴─────┐             ┌─────┴─────┐
   ┌───────┐  ┌──────────┐   ┌───────┐  ┌───────┐
   │Object │  │  Object  │   │ Track │  │ Trace │
   │Identity│ │Authentic.│   └───────┘  └───────┘
   └───────┘  └──────────┘
```

Object Identity	Object Authentication	Track	Trace
Is the Object identifier valid?	Does the Object have the expected covert and/or overt security features?	Where is the Object and where is it headed?	Where was the Object (Locations and Custodians)

This high level architecture view of safe and secure supply chain highlights two core elements:

Authentication: It covers two distinct areas; "object dientity" and "object authentication" associated with the key questions:

– Is the object identifier valid?

– Does the object have the expected covert and / or overt deterrents to prove authenticity and who is the authoritative and trusted source to verify the objects authenticity?

Pedigree: It includes key questions:

– Is the chain of custody intact?

– Where is the object and where is it headed?

– Where was the object and who has it now?

– Who is the trusted source for event data?

The Visibility Framework built upon global standards, supports this architecture by enabling the ability to know exactly where things are at any point in time (or where they have been) and why.

Visibility is not a business process or business application unto itself. Visibility is the capability that allows a company to achieve various business goals through seeing more relevant event-based information relating to business processes, then making use of that visibility data in business applications. It needs to be supported by traceability—the ability to trace one step up and track one step down in the supply chain. Tracing upstream is essentially being able to identify all objects received and from whom, relating them to internal traceability (i.e. a particular component from company x was used in product y with batch / lot number z). Tracking downstream is being able to track all outputs shipped and to whom.

Aforementioned visibility framework combined with other process standards such as the GS1 Global Traceability Standard (GTS) and the business messaging standard for Product Recall become very powerful tools to enable safe and secure supply chains.

Creating Visibility Framework

Visibility is a broad concept that relates to knowing where things are at any point in time and why they are there (or where they have been in the past). Visibility means leveraging a range of standards and business applications in order to see more event-based information relating to key business processes.

Many supply chain processes can be transformed through deeper, more accurate and rich visibility information. These processes could include improving overall supply chain accuracy, velocity and effectiveness, the management of inventory, product tracking and tracing, confirming the chain of custody and ownership of a product, product authentication and managing products returned by customers.

For an item or event to be visible in a business process, it must first be identified, its activity captured, and the information shared in a standard way so that all who need the information can understand it.

The globally accepted supply chain standards, developed by GS1 with active participation of Industry, provide a visibility framework by covering the following key areas:

- Identification standards that provide the foundation for globally unique identification items/events need to be visible
- Data standards that define the content and meaning of visibility data so that one supply chain party can understand data that it receives from another supply chain party.
- Interface standards that define how supply chain parties can interact with each other to exchange visibility data.

This open, interoperable and technology independent framework will enable organisations to make more informed and timely business decisions providing them with the answers related to what, when, where and why of an item or assets' movement. This in turn builds a solid foundation for product authentication, supply chain traceability, product recall and other visibility-driven business processes and applications.

Brands are protected against counterfeit by ensuring visibility at every level of the packaging and operational hierarchy level by using globally accepted supply chain standards as follows:

- Serialised identification of each component of the supply chain starting from the most elemental level, i.e., the very product that is sold in the marketplace upto the shipping units, supply chain partners and entities.

For example: all products of the same make and model carry a globally unique product identifier, GTIN (Global Trade Identification Number) and include a serial number along with the GTIN to form a serialized-GTIN or SGTIN.

Each physical shipping unit can be identified by using the Serial Shipping Container Code (SSCC) ID key.

Each supply chain entity can be identified using globally unique location identifier GLN (Global Location Number).

- Automatic data capture related to each component at any point of the supply chain encoding serialised identifications in proper data carriers.

  For example: GS1 DataMatrix is used primarily in pharmaceuticals, medical device manufacturing, and also in aerospace, this 2D (two-dimensional) barcode can hold large amounts of data like unique product identifier (GTIN), batch number, expiry data and serial number etc. in a relatively small space.

  Similarly EPC/RFID tags can also be used for encoding item level serialised identification data.

- Sharing information in the form master data, transactional data, and event data using standardised ways.

  For example: GS1 eCom standards for Electronic data interchange (EDI), Electronic Product Code Information Services (EPCIS), the Global Data Synchronization Network (GDSN) and other data pools can be used to share master, transactional and physical event data.

Addressing Challenges of Information Discovery

In the world of the Internet, information discovery is akin to using a search engine to locate information. The user does not know where the information they need is stored or replicated, but knows enough about the information to effectively search for it. Herein come concerns about trusted source of data and the appropriate way of communicating data

In any communication between two supply chain partners, two things must be present:
- A connection between the two parties; and
- An agreed protocol for communication.

Once a connection to a trading partner is established, the communication has to proceed in a way that is mutually agreeable and understood by the two parties. Use of global standards for identification, capture and data sharing enable to reduce the chance of friction between proprietary identification schema or order and acknowledgement transaction sets maintained by various supply chain partners.

In the supply chain, there is an analogous information requirement from the consumer or other interested party (regulators) which would allow the physical object to be determined as authentic or counterfeit.

Brand owners can satisfy this requirement by adopting several ways and technologies for product and packaging-marking, but none of them is wholly satisfactory.
- Packaging can be reproduced or altered by a counterfeiter;
- There is an impossibility to add services after the package is printed;
- If multiple marks are present, there is difficulty for users to know which one pertains to authentication for anti-counterfeiting purposes; and
- There is an impossibility to move services to another website without compromising the ability of users to interact with the services.

The one thing that a counterfeiter cannot change on a package is the unique code for this particular product pack that is globally unique serialised identifier. If such an identifier is tampered with, the entire (legitimate) downstream supply chain will not be able to handle the altered object identification and the counterfeit could be detected quickly.

Moreover, these globally unique keys help in locating parties in the supply chain that, in aggregate, have the trusted data associated with a set of attributes via a company owned source or a synchronized and trusted custodian source that could be a third-party authentication service provider.

BUILDING INTEROPERABLE SERVICES

With the massive growth in counterfeiting across all industry sectors, there is an increase in the number of solution providers with proprietary solutions as well as in-house developed solutions by brand owners resulting in the need for interoperability. Key to solving interoperability is a global standard and global infrastructure to enable it.

GS1 and ISO technical committee (PC247) are jointly working towards addressing the need for interoperability. The ISO standard will eventually define "WHAT" needs to occur in non-prescriptive terms while GS1 standards define the "HOW-TO" in prescriptive terms. Both are very complimentary.

The already ratified and industry developed standard called Object Naming Service (ONS) facilitates the need for interoperability of object identification and should be explored by a candidate to facilitate interoperable authentication services.

"Identity of an object and its "authenticity" are quite different but are bound tightly with the objects supply chain traceability and in some sectors, its pedigree (chain of custody).

ONS offers a pragmatic and feasible strategy to address this growing need. Existing and new solution providers could openly compete and innovate with their services with ONS providing interoperability and routing to the authoritative source and service end point for the brand authentication information. Brand owners or their solution providers retain full control of their authentication services including access rights and privileges, overall security, hosting, and user requirements. ONS could also be used to query blacklists, a record of cloned or compromised authentication codes, making it easier and faster to detect counterfeits.

Generally, ONS is about the successful discovery of relevant and trusted data and services associated with a globally unique Identification Key, for example: SGTIN for products, SSCCC for logistic units, can be used to look up data and services configured by the company that assigned it. This can be a very powerful tool for all stakeholders in the supply chain, including the manufacturer, distributor, importer, customs, retailer, market surveillance, and even the consumer.

BRINGING MOBILITY IN PRODUCT AUTHENTICATION

In this digital age, with over 4 billion mobile phone user worldwide, it has emerged as a powerful media for communication between brand owners, businesses and consumers. GS1 initiative named 'extended packaging'—literally extending the space of information sharing beyond the matter printed on the packaging into the digital world using mobile devices, facilitates instant authentication by linking consumers, businesses and regulators to a trusted source of product information.

It was introduced by the GS1 MobileCom group, a collaborative, neutral, global forum for all stakeholders interested in mobile commerce and mobile communications, to enable customers access all possible product information and related services, be it generic or personalized, by using the camera of a mobile device as a barcode/RFID reader. It facilitates instant product authentication as users can be connected automatically to an anti-counterfeiting application just by mobile scanning of a GS1 packaging. Counterfeiting is in existence since decades, several actions have been taken at national and international level to curb this menace, WHO created the first global initiative, known as the International Medical Products Anti-Counterfeiting Taskforce (IMPACT), to increase awareness and action in the fight against counterfeiting. It is working on five key areas:

- Legislative and regulatory framework (civil and penal aspects)
- Regulatory implementation (importation, distribution etc.)
- Enforcement (INTERPOL, World Customs Organization etc.)
- Communication (create awareness and foster cooperation)
- Technologies aiming to prevent, deter or detect counterfeit pharmaceuticals and medical devices.

This includes bar-coding, RFID and traceability in which global standards body GS1 is associated as a key work team member.

U.S. FDA's efforts are directed at securing the pharmaceutical supply chain through pedigree legislation which entails electronic track and trace system from manufacturing to point of dispensing, through all stages of distribution. The deadline date for implementation of such systems is 2015. EFPIA (European Federation of Pharmaceutical Industries and Associations) is looking at mass serialisation of pharmaceuticals as the way to detect counterfeits and is looking at implementation by Industry within next four to five years. EFPIA is thereby promoting authentication as the best approach to detect counterfeits in the supply chain and has proven their position with a successful pilot in Sweden involving all stakeholders.

Various coding solutions have been implemented by Member States in Europe, each with their own objectives and motivation. The coexistence of these different systems constitutes an obstacle to enhanced tracking and tracing of medicines at EU level and adds production and associated costs. This has led EFPIA to recommend the implementation of a standardized identification solution for pharmaceutical products across Europe.

EFPIA advocates the Global standards GS1 Data Matrix bar code with a unique product identifier (GTIN), batch number, expiry data and serial number, as the minimum data standard.

Conclusion

Currently several overt and covert technologies are used as brand protection techniques by manufacturers and brand owners. Most of such techniques are brand owners specific and cannot be easily authenticated by an outsider and consumers and at times requires specialized training.

Counterfeiting being a potential element to damage global economy, jeopardize public safety and undermine legitimate businesses, a global approach is required to ensure secure and safe supply chains. GS1 as a global not-for-profit standards body can facilitate this approach.

Visibility Framework built upon GS1 standards provides important capabilities to improve collaboration, transparency, efficiency, security and visibility in the supply chain. A key component of the visibility framework that enables real-time sharing of information is the application interface standard called EPCIS, which is both industry and technology neutral.

It was created and designed by industry to fit within existing enterprise and security environments as a supplement to existing enterprise information systems. It reduces complexity, the cost of implementation and integration while facilitating improved trading partner collaboration and visibility: EPCIS allows organizations to focus more on how to use the information than how to get information.

GS1 standards were developed by industry for industry. They are consensus driven, voluntary and neutral to technologies and implementations. By adopting GS1 Standards as the foundation for business processes and interoperability, companies of all sizes can speak a common language, connect seamlessly and leverage the power of information to their businesses. Diverse industries are able to adapt easily, and use these standards to transform the way they do business, following in the footsteps of industry leaders who envision the future and exemplify industry's best practices.

NEED FOR AMENDING LAWS TO CHECK COUNTERFEITING

Amendments that need to be made in the trademark's act-1999.

It is suggested that in this new Trade Marks Act 1999, power of search and seizure should be given to the Police Officer now below the rank of SI instead of DSP! ACP (as in the case of the Copy Right Act).

It is suggested that the requirement of the opinion of the registrar Trade Marks about the infringement of the Trade mark Act should be dispensed with as this will minimize the possibility of leakage of information and expedite action under the Trade Marks Act.

II: Steps to be taken to check counterfeiting at the Production level

The Govt. departments that can be approached in this regard are the Excise department of the Central Govt and the, VAT/ Commercial Tax and Excise department of the state govt. But before we approach them it would be necessary that we identify the commodity and know about the magnitude of the problem, based on the feed-back from the affected Industries.

In FICCI, a database is required to be created which will compile and collate important statistics relating to counterfeiting and smuggling. Available data will have to be obtained from the affected Industries as well as from the enforcement agencies like Police, Customs, Excise, VAT, Commercial Tax Departments etc.,

After obtaining inputs from the affected industries, we may have to send a one-time comprehensive proposal to the Law Ministry and other concerned Ministries/Departments for required amendments to be carried out with a view to make IPR laws more effective.

Meetings with the senior officers of Police, Customs and other concerned Govt. Departments should be held once we are prepared with the basic information compiled on the basis of the feed-back to be received from the affected industries. Such meetings will also have to be held besides New Delhi at other important places as well, such as those, indicated above.

With a view to expedite judicial proceedings; meetings could be held with the Law Ministry and we can make out a case for setting up of separate courts for dealing with the IPR related cases. In this regard necessary data on the pendency of court cases at different levels will be required.

> The deadline date for implementation of such system is 2015. EFPIA (European Federation of Pharmaceutical Industries and Associations) is looking at mass serialisation of pharmaceuticals as the way to detect counterfeits and is looking at implementation by Industry within next four to five years. EFPIA is thereby promoting authentication as the best approach to detect counterfeits in the supply chain and has proven their position with a successful pilot in Sweden involving all stakeholders.
>
> Various coding solutions have been implemented by Member States in Europe, each with their own objectives and motivation. The coexistence of these different systems constitutes an obstacle to enhanced tracking and tracing of medicines at EU level and adds production and associated costs. This has led EFPIA to recommend the implementation of a standardized identification solution for pharmaceutical products across Europe.
>
> EFPIA advocates the Global standards GS1 Data Matrix bar code with a unique product identifier (GTIN), batch number, expiry data and serial number, as the minimum data standard.

> **Indian initiatives to combat counterfeit using global standards**
>
> As part of the constant efforts to streamline the procurement and tracking of drugs, the **Ministry of Health and Family Welfare (MoHFW), Government of India** has made barcodes using GS1 standards compulsory for all drugs purchased by the Government of India through its divisions for various programs.

Directorate General of Foreign Trade (DGFT) has also mandated the use of barcoding and GS1 standards for export consignments of drugs. (http://dgftcom.nic.in/exim/2000/pn/pn10/pn5910.htm). The recent movement of Indian pharmaceutical sector towards adoption of GS1 standards and barcoding for track and trace and authentication of medicines would provide enhanced safety to consumers worldwide.

Delhi State Excise Department advanced with development of a comprehensive IT application to monitor movement of alcoholic beverages from manufacturing to Retail outlets using serialised GS1 BarCodes. Through use of serialised GS1 BarCodes on alcoholic beverages, product authentication would become possible, providing assurance to consumers against counterfeit activities.

Contributed by GS1 India

GS1 India is a not-for-profit standards body set up by the Ministry of Commerce, Govt. of India and leading Chambers comprising CII, FICCI, ASSOCHAM, IMC, FIEO besides BIS, IIP, Spices Board and APEDA to educate and assist Indian Industry in adoption of global standards used in supply chain management for facilitating faster movement of physical goods and related information flow electronically. It is affiliated to GS1, Brussels which oversees a network of over 110 GS1 organisations worldwide.

For more information, visit www.gs1india.org.

CHAPTER 2

Challenges Facing the Indian Manufacturing Industry

Our immediate neighbors have indeed mastered the art of producing unimaginable numbers of wide ranging products and selling in different parts of the world at prices cheaper than the prevailing rates in that particular country, simply put its called 'Dumping'. This leads to massive losses to the domestic suppliers, impacts employment and dents the exchequer. India has been at the receiving end of an aggressive dumping policy, this coupled with the recent recession has led to India filing the maximum anti dumping cases against some of its neighbors at the WTO. Many of our surrounding countries have increasingly resorted to all conceivable methods of selling their products to India at dirt cheap prices causing massive bleeding to the domestic producers. India's infrastructure does not permit it as yet to observe huge economies of a scale like some of our neighbors. Having this competitive advantage, our neighbor is bolstering itself by diverting its products to India, causing irreparable damage to the Indian domestic market. These goods are 10-70 per cent cheaper than their Indian counterparts and the flood of such products into India has negatively impacted companies across sectors, this has had a significant impact at a time when the demand is already low due to the global slowdown, this has been clearly stated by a survey conducted by FICCI.

India shares a massive common border with its neighbor, they are indeed immediate neighbors, providing passage to counterfeit, contraband products into India, sometimes directly and sometimes indirectly. At one stage India was inundated by cheap mobile phones manufactured across the border, the sheer numbers made the Indian government take note. These penetrated the major cities and small towns alike. When people saw cheap, reasonably qualitative alternatives these phones ate into the sale of major international and national companies alike. Finally the government declared all phones without an IMEI number to be illegal and the sale of such mobiles was brought down. However it's a known fact that in a majority of small towns these mobiles are still very much preferred. In fact, this has curtailed the growth of not just the domestic mobile companies but the spread of known international mobile brands to many parts of the country.

One of the Countries has cleverly targeted the Acrylic Yarn sector in manufacturing. The market share of imports from the country have risen from 8.36 per cent in 1998-99 to 27.37 per cent in 2000-01. These imports have been made from our neighbor at dumped prices since the normal value determined on constructed cost of production is significantly higher than the export price. These dumped imports have been causing serious injury to the domestic Industry resulting in stagnation and decline. As mentioned before, Counterfeit/Contraband goods are easily finding a way into India through the rather porous borders. These products are much cheaper than those which are legally imported and thus cause losses to the domestic importer.

Even today chargers of brands like Nokia, top laptop brands bear the stamp of our neighboring countries. It's this art of 'counterfeit' products from various countries which is making India a major victim. That's not all, sectors like Cigarette, Rubber, Steel, Auto parts and Aluminium have been bombarded by such goods and where our neighbor has taken the domestic market by storm. There is no comparison with our neighbor as it is one of the top economic powers of the world and India which is quickly trying to catch up.

Despite having a world class set up in the Madras Rubber Factory(MRF), neighboring country sold tyres in India at 30 per cent cheaper rate than the cost of tyres produced in India. Obviously, for a country where much of its population is below the comfort level and where money is dear, there is an immediate attraction for such cheap alternatives which are without doubt 'counterfeit'. So, it's hardly surprising that about 80 per cent of the demand for tyres is met with cheap foreign imports whose quality is suspect.

The state of the Auto parts Industry is not too different, despite being a part of the 'Sunrise Industries' which have provided a major boost to the Indian economy, our neighbors have penetrated this sector as well. The share of crankshaft in such imports for one of the countries for example increased from 2.3 per cent in the first half of 2008 to 15.75 per cent in the following quarter of 2008. Stainless steel products imported too have witnessed a consistent annual increase by 20-30 per cent since 2006. The imports of Aluminium and chemical products from our neighbors have increased nearly three times in the recent years.

The list only expands, after dumping silk, man-made fibres and chemicals, India has observed the growing presence of our neighbors 'cotton voile' fabric in India. India has lodged a complaint on the basis that despite our neighbor being a net importer of cotton and having a good stock-to-use ratio, it is exporting cotton voile to India at prices much lower than the production cost. This dumping of cotton fabric has added to the problems of the Textiles sector, which is already burdened by the recent increase in cotton prices.

In 2009, India initiated a probe into the alleged dumping of 'Sodium Tripoly Phosphate', a chemical used in household cleaning products, human foodstuffs and animal feeds by our neighbor after its detrimental impact on the domestic industry came to light. This was finalized recently in June, 2011, when it was decided that the restrictive duty on the import of the chemical would be for a period of five years.

India's Directorate General of Anti-dumping and Allied Duties investigated a complaint by L&T against imported tire presses and declared that they had increased to 7 per cent of the total volume of India's domestic tire press market in 2007-08, compared to just 0.6 per cent in 2004-05.

India recently imposed an anti-dumping duty of Rs 1 lakh, 55 thousand per lakh unit on import of sewing machine needles to protect domestic players from cheap shipments. Just like Sodium Tripoly Phosphate, this anti dumping duty will be applicable for a span of five years. In 2009, the Commerce Ministry in its preliminary findings showed that the domestic Industry suffered serious material injury due to "dumping" of Synchronous Digital Hierarchy (SDH) transmission equipment from our neighbors and had to step in to immediately impose provisional anti-dumping duty on its imports. The complaint was lodged by India's Tejas networks charging that the importers were undercutting their prices, leading to massive losses and pressure on local manufacturers.

Recently, India also suffered a hard hit from one of its neighbours in the Ceramic Glazed Tile market, so much that a provisional anti dumping duty of Rs 137 per square meter on those imported from that country is being considered. The Directorate General of Anti-dumping and Allied Duties has asked the Commerce ministry for this to be imposed, as the domestic manufacturers were being battered.

Despite all these measures, the Indian Manufacturers are having a tough time battling products from our neighbors which in some manner or the other restrict their growth prospects. This not only stubs profits and growth but also impacts the employment scenario in the entire country. The sheer range of products and their presence in most parts of India is a matter of grave concern and requires immediate attention. We cannot change our neighbors but we certainly need to change our approach to make a difference in the mind set of all stakeholders so that we collectively take steps which will make us proud of the 'Made in India' label, augmenting nation building.

CHAPTER 3

Enforcement of Anti-Counterfeit and Anti-Smuggling Laws

COUNTERFEIT

Different countries use different definitions of counterfeit goods. However appropriately addressing counterfeiting issues largely depends on what the definition of counterfeit is. While all legal definitions of the term include a violation of intellectual property rights, whether the definition includes any additional elements is matter for debate. The World Health Organization defines counterfeit medicines to be deliberately and fraudulently mislabeled with respect to identity or source. Some countries require that counterfeits are manufactured on a commercial scale. Whether a good is counterfeit when it only infringes IP rights, intentionally infringes IP rights, or must be produced on a commercial scale in order to be a counterfeit good may drastically change IP enforcement regimes.

IMPORTANT FACTORS RESPONSIBLE FOR COUNTERFEITING IN INDIA

- **Price Differentials:** significant price differences amongst neighbouring countries.
- **Tax Arbitrage:** high taxed products provide tax arbitrage opportunity to unsubscribe dealers.

- **Nature of the Product:** products having higher margin, easy to transport and having ready market are more prone to illicit trade
- **Organised Crime Magnet:** a major source of income for organized crime, funding terrorism
- **Ineffective Control:** weak surveillance, weak regulatory framework, lack of stringent actions etc.
- **Consumer Attitudes:** to the consumers, buying the product duty free, casts the seller in the light of benefactor rather than a criminal (Robin Hood Syndrome)

IMPACT OF ILLICIT TRADE

A. The impact of illicit trade on Government is as follows:
   - Undermine tax base and loss of tax revenue
   - Weaken government health and fiscal objectives
   - Exposes consumer to unregulated product
   - Encourages widespread criminality
   - Stifles innovation
B. The impact of illicit trade on Business is as follows:
   - Disrupts the market for suppliers, distributors and retailers
   - Undermines investment in distribution network
   - Damages Brand Equity
   - Fosters counterfeit production
C. The impact of illicit trade on Ordinary Citizens is as follows:
   - Loss of employment
   - Link to organized crime and terrorism
   - Health threat from substandard products

MAJOR SECTORS AFFECTED BY THE COUNTERFEITING IN INDIA

- Drugs and Medicines: 15% - 20% of total market
- Fast Moving Consumer Goods (FMCG): 8% - 10%

- Auto Spares: 37%
- Music Industry: 40%
- IT/Software: 80%
- Soft Drinks: 10%
- Cosmetics and Toiletries: 10% - 30%

THE LEGAL POSITION IN INDIA

The primary legislations in India, dealing with counterfeiting are the Trademarks Act 1999, the Copyright Act 1957 and the Customs Act 1962.

The **Trademarks Act 1999** provides remedies for the infringement of a registered trademark, as well as a common law remedy of passing off to protect against infringement of an unregistered trademark. Section 27(2) recognizes the common law remedy of passing off against any person dealing in counterfeit goods. Section 29 mentions the various acts that amount to the infringement of a registered trademark. Section 135 provides for civil remedies in case of either infringement or passing off. These remedies include injunction, damages, delivery-up and rendition of accounts. Section 103 provides for criminal remedies such as imprisonment of up to 3 years and fines of up to Rs.2,00,000 in case of counterfeiting.

Section 51 of the **Copyright Act 1957** envisages the various acts that amount to the infringement of copyright vested with the owner. Further Section 53 restricts the importation of copies which would infringe copyright. The act also provides both civil and criminal remedies against software counterfeiting Section 55 provides for civil remedies by way of injunction, damages, rendition of accounts and delivery up. As far as criminal remedies are concerned, Section 64 empowers the police to seize all counterfeit software copies, while Section 63 provides for imprisonment of up to 3 years and fines up to Rs.2,00,000 in case of infringement abatement.

Section 11 of the **Customs Act 1962** empowers the customs officials to prohibit the importation and exportation of goods in order to protect copyrights and trademarks. Goods bearing false Trade Marks or false descriptions are prohibited from being imported into India under the Customs Act, 1962 and when imported are liable to detention or confiscation. In addition, a new customs recordal system has been introduced through the Intellectual Property Rights (Imported Goods) Enforcement Rules 2007 to strengthen border enforcement with the objective of preventing the entry of counterfeit goods into the country.

'ANTON PILLER' ORDERS AND 'JOHN DOE' ORDERS

In addition to the extensive police powers under the Copyright Act mentioned above, plaintiffs have other, equally intrusive powers at their disposal. In the past decade it has become common for copyright owners and owners-associations to employ civil procedure to emulate the same kind of invasiveness. This is done via the mechanism of so-called 'Anton Piller' orders-orders obtained unilaterally 'ex-parte' (in the absence of the defendant) from civil courts which permit court-appointed officers, accompanied by representatives of the plaintiffs themselves, to search premises and seize evidence without prior warning to the defendant. Frequently, courts have also issued 'John Doe' orders-orders to search and seize against unnamed/unknown defendants—which virtually translates into untrammelled powers in the hands of the plaintiffs, aided by court-appointed local commissioners, to raid any premises they set their eyes on.

Important Issues to be addressed in the Enforcement of the Anti-Counterfeiting Laws

Lack of interest in prosecution: In many a cases it has been observed that the victim is interested only in the first part of the case such as seizure of counterfeited/smuggled goods and the arrest of the accused persons. The victim feels that his purpose has been achieved and is satisfied with this initial action and withdraws from the rest of the prosecution exercise in the interest of his business. For achieving the full objective of the law, the copyright holder and the law enforcement agency should work in close coordination with clear objective of getting maximum punishment to the infringer.

Powers of search and seizure: In case of the Copyright Act 1957, the powers of search and seizure are vested with "any police officer not below the rank of a Sub-inspector" while under the Trade Mark Act 1999, Sec. 115(4), the powers for search and seizure are vest in "any officer not below the rank of Dy. S.P." which is an impediment in the enforcement of the law due to limited availability of the officers in this rank. This anomaly needs to be addressed appropriately and as in case of the Copyright Act1957 the powers of search and seizure may be given to "any officer not below the rank of Sub-inspector of police."

Opinion of the Registrar: Further under sub-section 4 of Sec. 115 of the Trade Marks Act 1999, the police officer, before making any search and seizure shall obtain the opinion of the Registrar on facts involved in the offences relating to trade mark and shall abide by the opinion so obtained. This provision makes the procedure lengthy and the purpose of search and seizure may become infructuous because of the possibility of leakage of information is more and instant/prompt action is not possible. There will be sufficient time for pirates to remove the infringed goods and the purpose of raid will be defeated.

Status of Enforcement in the Capital

It has been claimed by many that the metropolitan cities are hubs of counterfeit business, both in manufacturing as well as trading and that 70 per cent of the counterfeit business is centered in

Delhi. However it does not show in the figures of the crime reported in Delhi. Following chart indicates a different story. (All India figures are not available).

Year	No. of cases reported under Copyright Act	No. of cases reported under Trademark Act
2005	202	24
2006	189	16
2007	147	03
2008	145	26
2009	134	47
2010	46	22
2011*	30	37

*Up to 30 June

This indicates that the traders are not in favour of reporting the incidents of infringements to the law enforcement authority. This could be for various reasons. It could be because of the time involved and cumbersome delay in the investigation and the trial of the cases or it could be due to their business interests that the traders want to avoid the judicial method to check this menace to their business. It is also true that most of the good brands have engaged their own private brand protection teams who continuously conduct survey in the markets and take measures to protect their business interest.

This would certainly require streamlining our process of reporting, investigation, and speeding up of trial of cases to win the trust of the trading community on one hand and the resolve of the trading community to take recourse to do their best to get the infringers prosecuted in the overall national interest.

Measures to be Adopted

India has adequate IP laws and an effective judicial system in place to tackle counterfeiting. However much has still to be done to curb the problem, in particular with regard to software piracy. To counter piracy, a four-pronged approach should be adopted.

- Firstly efforts are to be made to increase IP awareness throughout the country. This could be achieved through education programs, newspapers, circulars and pamphlets organized or distributed by government agencies and non-governmental agencies.
- Secondly, it is of paramount importance that the legal fraternity and the enforcement agencies are fully aware and equipped to deal with the various aspects of IP law. This could be achieved by organizing training programs for judges and police personnel on a regular basis.
- Thirdly, efforts to speed up trials should be made; this would enhance the efficiency of the legal system by ensuring the early prosecution of counterfeiters and pirates.
- Lastly, more specialised police cells are required to be created to deal with IP and other economic offences in various cities around the country. Existing specialist departments with meager human resource and inadequate logistic support are not sufficient in view of the volume of IP violations. Further the enforcement personnel should be given adequate powers.
- Further, the courts are to be equipped with modern technologies to handle carious IP issues more effectively.

CHAPTER 4

Curbing Counterfeiting Through Taxation

The wise minister of the Mauryan king had advised that since all undertakings (of the State) depends on finance, the king should pay foremost attention to the treasury. The relevance of his opinion has not reduced during the last twenty-three centuries. The advice of the wise, throughout the ages, has been followed by the governments with sincerity for raising revenue from the citizens.

In present times, the need for more revenue is much greater than in the past. This is because, now, the State is into many such activities which were not the State's responsibilities earlier. In the past, the State's role in activities relating to public welfare was minimal. Now, it is substantial. There is hardly any aspect of the citizen's life which remains untouched from the State's intervention. The State always had the responsibility of providing protection from external threat and maintaining peace at home by establishing rule of law. What has been added now is that, in the present time, the State has its role, more or less, in all activities relating to public welfare also. To discharge these many functions, the requirement of revenue has increased.

Taxations experts in the Finance Ministry remain engaged in carrying out continuous research to find out ways and means to augment revenue, and in the process, not cause any undue hardship to the taxpayers, following the old wisdom that tax should be collected like bee which takes honey from flowers without hurting them.

An important consideration which influences taxation decisions is that those with greater capacity to do so should pay more. However, there is no escape for anyone from paying at least some tax to the government irrespective of his/her income level, i.e., whether the person's income is above or below the line of Rs. 22/29 per day. With this objective in view, whereas, rates of direct taxes like income tax, corporation tax, wealth tax, etc, depend on the income of the taxpayers, the incidence of indirect taxes such as union and state excise, service tax, customs, vat, octroi, purchase tax, etc, falls on everyone to the extent he/she has the need and capacity to consume goods and services.

In case of indirect taxes also, although it is kept in mind that on the goods and services consumed mainly by the people in the lower income category, the burden of taxes is less. But in view of distortions in economy resulting from exemptions and multiple rates of taxation, decisions are often taken in favour of uniformity in rates and minimising, if not eliminating, exemptions.

Another important factor which influences, to a large extent, the decision for augmentation of revenue is that if the people, in spite of statutory warnings, are determined not to give up their self-injurious habits like consuming alcohol, tobacco products, etc, then they must make higher contribution to the State exchequer also.

The State's policy seems to be to make these sin products costlier so as to curb their consumption , and also, to get higher revenue from such goods. This line of thinking about revenue collection has many ramifications. It is debatable whether making such products costlier would, in fact, result in reducing their production and consumption. As the experience has shown, it has not. The other alternative for the State may be to try to prohibit manufacture and consumption of such goods. But this too has its own enforcement and integrity linked issues, hence, such a measure is unlikely to be successful. Also, it is difficult for the government to take other alternative measures to compensate for the huge loss of revenue as a result of prohibition/ban on these goods.

Yet another aspect linked to higher rates of taxation on such goods is that the present system encourages activities like counterfeiting, piracy, tax-evasion, and smuggling which have serious negative impact on the economy. This happens because those who, due to the compulsion of their habit, must buy the goods they need and to that extent, their requirements, builds up a pressure for making such goods available at affordable lower prices. Consumers of these goods are from all income groups including those who are also below the poverty line. This illegal activity gets facilitated due to inadequacy of legal provisions to deal with it and also by the obvious laxity in enforcement of the existing laws. Further, the counterfeiters and smugglers, in their effort to make such goods available at cheaper affordable prices, while not compromising with the profit which they must make, manufacture similar goods which invariably are of sub-standard quality. As a result, the situation which has emerged is that on one hand, the government loses revenue due to illicit production and consumption, and on the other, the consumers whom the government wishes to protect, actually get exposed to greater health hazards. This is so because consumption of good quality products of even sin goods would be much less harmful to health than the counterfeited sub- standard products in the manufacturing of which quality has been compromised.

As we are aware, the different authorities like police, customs, etc, responsible to check counterfeiting have always many other more pressing priorities, and hence, they are unable to give the desired emphasis to this aspect of their work. The available information suggests that although counterfeiting activity is rising fast with the passage of time, the preparedness of the enforcement agencies more or less either remains the same or improves only at slow pace. According to an assessment, during the last two decades itself, the counterfeiting activity has increased by one hundred times. The situation is alarming. It calls for immediate attention of all concerned to take serious note of the same and deal with it effectively. There is hardly any product which has remained unaffected from the ingenuity of the counterfeiters. Higher the rates of taxes on any goods, the greater would be the profit involved in counterfeiting the product, greater is the risk to health of people, and also, greater the loss of revenue through evasion.

In this scenario, it would be prudent that while deciding about the rates of indirect taxes like excise, vat, customs, etc, on items which are subjected to high rates of taxes like alcohol, tobacco products, etc, besides other points, it may also be borne in mind that very high rates of taxes on these goods provides undesired incentive to the activities like counterfeiting and smuggling, and consequently, make the people much more vulnerable to the ill-effects of spurious goods. This, in a way, also results in a dichotomy that although people are warned against consumption of such goods, they actually land in a situation where a sizeable portion of the counterfeit goods they consume are much more harmful to them than the genuine products. The concerns of health can always be better addressed by undertaking mass awareness campaigns on a sustained basis. In this area, there exists wide gap which is confirmed by such reports that in India, fifty percent of smokers to-day do not know that consumption of tobacco products is harmful for health. Hence, the plea that high rates of taxation on sin products is justified in view of its impact on curbing consumption of such goods does not carry much weight. There is a need to strike the right balance between the requirement of revenue on one hand and protection of people from the ill-effects of counterfeited sub-standard products, on the other. As a proper public policy measure, the balance may not be tilted in favour of one at the cost of the other.

It would be desirable to take this aspect also into consideration at the time of taking decisions about rates of indirect taxes on such products.

Even today, as in the fourth century BC, while collecting honey, the bee does not cause any harm to flowers. The present day governments may also continue to make effort not to cause dispensable injury to taxpayers in the process of collecting revenue as it tried to do in the past.

P. C. Jha
Consultant, FICCI-CASCADE;
Ex-Chairman, CBEC

Chapter 5
Industries Affected by Counterfeiting

COUNTERFEIT SPARE PARTS

Aarti Gupta is a Bank Manager and drives her car to work. She was driving herself to work on 15th April 2011 and while coming down the Defence Colony flyover in New Delhi, she suddenly saw heavy traffic in front and wanted to slow down but to her horror, however hard she pressed the brakes, the car was not responding. Aarti tried to press the brakes repeatedly but to no avail. She started screaming but by then she had crashed into a bus. Fortunately Aarti was wearing her seat belts and escaped with minor bruises but her car had major damage in front. Aarti called her husband Nitin and told him about the accident. Nitin was very surprised as he had got the car serviced at a neighbourhood private workshop only 3 days back and had been told that the brake linings and the brake pads were replaced. He suspected foul play and was livid that the accident happened.

Such incidents are not uncommon but occur quite regularly in India as fake automotive parts are readily available at cheap rates and we all fall prey to them in trying to save a few hundred rupees, least realizing that we could endanger ourselves and our near and dear ones. *A study indicates that approximately 20% of the total road accidents in India can be attributed to use of counterfeit products.*

Fake automotive parts market in India is estimated to be around Rs. 2500 crores of which approximately 35 per cent of the total auto parts sold in the country are counterfeit or fake and not only endanger consumers but also escape the tax net causing a loss of Rs. 250 crores to the exchequer.

Reasons for High Piracy in India	
Cheap	Most of the replica counterfeited / pirated products are sold at 40-45 per cent lesser value than the original market rate. Customers are tempted to purchase these owing to the price factor and therefore, there exists a high demand for them.
Availability	These counterfeit parts are easily available in the market
Limited Knowledge	Usually a layman with limited knowledge would fall prey to these bogus products owing to the cheap or discounted prices
Product Packaging	These products are packaged just like the original products and are then sold to unsuspecting customers
Poor Law Enforcement	Enforcement of laws against piracy needs to be strengthened

What can we do about it and whether such illegal trade should be allowed to function in the country? We also must remember that such illegal trade generates wealth for anti-social elements of the society who in turn fuel various activities like insurgency, terrorism, etc. and this vicious cycle of vice needs to be broken and as consumers, we need to be vigilant.

A walk around the Crawford Market in Mumbai or Palika Bazar in New Delhi will throw the following startling results:

Brands	Avg. Price of original in Rs.	Avg. Price of Fake in Rs.
Watches		
Rolex	3 lakh	3000
TAG Heuer	70,000	2000
Shoes and Apparel		
Nike	2500	750
Adidas	3000	800

Federation of Indian Chambers of Commerce and Industry (FICCI) has recently launched a committee on anti-smuggling and counterfeit activities destroying the economy (CASCADE) which is mobilizing the industry in all sectors not only in automotive sector to join hands in a drive to meet the challenges posed by such illegal activities and to raise awareness among all stakeholders.

Regulatory Framework

Category of Law	Legislation	Remedy
IPR	Copyrights Act, Trademark Act, Patents Act, Design Act	Infringement Suit, Police takes cognizance on complaint
Civil	Civil Procedure Code	Civil Suit, Injunctive relief
Criminal	IPC	Imprisonment

For curbing this menace the law enforcement agencies have made available various channels for consumers to report such crimes i.e. www.copconnect.in by the Mumbai Police. Complaints can also be lodged with the tax authorities such as Central Excise and VAT authorities on their website www.cbec.gov.in/grievance.htm. The automobile component industries as well as the original equipment manufacturers have been conducting various drives to arrest this issue; however, they are up against the huge market dominated by people having muscle and money power to throw out any attempts made.

Smuggling and counterfeiting of tobacco products is a big problem being faced by all the nations, with varying scales. This illicit trade is a serious international problem, which requires an aggressive and coordinated response from governments and enforcement agencies.

There are several dimensions to this problem of illicit trade of tobacco products:
- As smuggled and counterfeit tobacco products evade policy framework on tobacco products.
- Encourages Anti-social elements to take charge of business channels resulting in organized crime syndicates.
- It is a lose-lose situation for government, legitimate industry and consumers.

Tax arbitrage across various countries, act as primary stimulant towards smuggling of cigarettes, whereby smugglers evade the duties and taxes and move cigarettes from lower tax to higher tax countries. The smugglers smuggle cigarettes into a country where they can make the highest profit, and this should be a country where tax is a high proportion of the price. As the tax component in cigarettes is high in India these days, smugglers are flooding the Indian market with foreign-made cigarettes.

Reports suggest that non-duty paid sales are a major concern for India, with some reports suggesting that 14 per cent of total cigarette consumption as the size of illicit trade in the case of Indian market.[1]

- Euromonitor report of 2010 also points out that India is one of the top 15 countries for illicit cigarettes consumption, accounting for 3.3 per cent of the total worldwide illicit cigarette consumption.[2] This report also point out that India is one of key illicit destination market for selling smuggled cigarettes.
- This report has pointed out that there has been a sharp growth of 57.7 per cent over the period of 2004-2009 in the illicit cigarette consumption in India , and tax driven price hikes in 2008 has caused the cheaper products from neighboring countries to increase the illicit consumption. The report cites another study, Combating Counterfeiting - Brand Protection, commissioned by the Associated Chambers of Commerce and Industry of India, which has pegged the cost of contraband in India at Rs. 1,700 crore per annum and is threatening the livelihoods of five million tobacco farmers. The worst part is that illicit consumption is forecasted to continue to rise over the next five years.

India is already a signatory to FCTC framework and tobacco smuggling as an important issue has also been recognized by FCTC. It specifically recommends actions to be taken to eliminate

---

[1] A report by Bloomberg Philanthropies and the Bill and Melinda Gates Foundation, 2009 with a cross reference to Euromonitor International Country market insight. India. March 2005.

[2] Illicit trade in tobacco products—A world view, July 2010, A report by Euromonitor International.

tobacco smuggling in Article 15. Some issues which continue to pose a great challenge to all of us, are:

1. While India has taken a progressive step of banning the FDI is tobacco sector, it requires some additional steps to make the steps really effective. As mentioned above, smuggling of cigarettes offer a big opportunity to unscrupulous elements to gain huge profits by avoiding paying duties and taxes, which form a large component in price paid by the consumer.

2. Foreign companies continue to promote their brands in India through various promotional activities. Such activities create a brand recall in the minds of consumers, and creates a demand in the minds of consumers, on the basis of perceived superiority of imported foreign and big brands. Once this kind of demand for their brands are established, various illicit channels become operative to fulfill the demand. When India has enacted a separate law "Cigarettes and Other Tobacco Products (Prohibition of Advertisement and Regulation of Trade and Commerce, Production, Supply and Distribution) Act, 2003" which prohibits the advertisements and controls every other aspect of cigarette trade and commerce, there is no basis to continue to allow free flow of capital for this purpose.

3. Many multi-national companies continue to press the government for opening up the market for foreign investments in this sector. Entry of such big multinationals in this sector will only mean the entry of bigger players, with deeper pockets, which will result in driving the tobacco consumption upwards in India and undermining the entire effort of government towards tobacco control.

4. Complicity of some large scale players in actively promoting smuggling has also been cited in some reports. This report by Collin et al., has identified several key attributes of such operations, key observations regarding some important attributes are being reproduced below:

(a) **Entering the closed markets:** A key factor of particular importance to contraband in Asia is that several target markets were effectively closed to legitimate imports, leaving smuggling as the sole means of ensuring the availability of international brand cigarettes. These companies lobbied to open these markets to create greater market salience.

(b) **Pressure for market opening:** Smuggling in Asia has also been used as a means of exerting political leverage to secure market opening. In Thailand, for example, exploitation of contraband was presented as part of a broader strategy to undermine Thailand's ban on imports.

(c) **Undermining regulations:** The ability to undermine effective health policy has been critical to the value of smuggling to tobacco companies. Successful orchestration of increased contraband flows with media pressure to curb taxation policy has occurred in countries such as Canada, Sweden, and the UK. Several documents of one of the largest tobacco companies, provide more detailed accounts of how the reliable availability of smuggled cigarettes contributed to efforts to influence public policy. In Bangladesh, documents suggest that this company exerted substantial control over flows of contraband cigarettes and presented such flows to the government as proof of the need to reverse increased excise.

(d) **Running legal business to support contraband:** Capacity to exploit contraband flows was enhanced by the seemingly widespread practice of coordinating operations across legal and illegal channels. In several markets a small legal operation was established to provide protective cover for smuggled sales, hence the term "umbrella operations." A token legal presence enabled marketing and promotional activities to be undertaken in support of contraband. In other contexts the dividing line between legal and illegal business could be effectively blurred; "'legal' imports could hide large scale transit activity." Documents demonstrate that ostensibly legitimate duty free sales have provided an effective means of supplying smuggled cigarettes.

5. Duty Free Sales: Sale of foreign brands of cigarettes through duty free shops has also been identified as one of the concerned areas not only in FCTC but also in other reports. The fundamental argument against sale of cigarettes through duty free channel remains an issue of the public health. In the light of public health concerns associated with higher tobacco consumption, there is no basis of giving any duty exemptions on sale of cigarettes through this channel, when that is not available to other channels. Possibility of duty free channels acting as one of the sources of leakage and feeding the illegitimate supply-chains has been well reported. Infact FCTC is considering recommending a ban on duty free sales of cigarettes, which often get diverted into illicit trade. Such a ban is already under consideration by many governments around the world.

6. Another impact of illicit trade is on the effort which government is making towards tobacco control in India, e.g. India has enacted very stringent pictorial warning regime on cigarettes. The same has not been enacted by all the countries. While the legitimate operators from India are bound to comply with these smuggled cigarettes, originating from other countries, which have either still not enacted framework or are not even signatories to FCTC framework, will continue to be available in market to consumers.

This means that consumers will always be having a choice of two types of cigarettes, one which has a statutory warning and is costlier, and another which doesn't have any warning printed on it and is also cheaper. The results of such a scenario are not difficult to predict.

7. Illicit trade in cigarettes has often been reported to have linkages with organized crime, even terrorist organizations. Smuggling being a criminal and illegal activity, there is every possibility that it uses the same distribution chain and networks which organized criminals or terrorists organizations use. Many

cases of this nature have been reported in international press.[4] This was also referred by Douglas Bettcher, Coordinator of framework convention team of WHO's tobacco free initiative, when he made a statement "We know that international drug cartels have some links with terrorists but now proofs are emerging of illegal tobacco smugglers links with terrorist outfits…."[5] It can't be worse for India, as it is already facing the issue of global terrorist outfits operating here.

Measures taken by the government have been centered around punitive taxation, as the price has been the primary mechanism employed. But the danger of using this approach is that it can possibly turn smokers towards consuming illicit products and end up as being counter-productive to the purpose for which it is deployed. These higher prices also make the illicit trade, because of it's high margins, more attractive for large scale smugglers.

Illicit trade also completely undermines the efforts made by government towards controlling tobacco consumption, because it makes the non-duty paid cigarettes an attractive option for consumers—especially the younger consumers, as well as smugglers, while everyone else, i.e. the governments and the society, end up as losers, with public health being the worst hit.

Illicit cigarettes that enter or are sold in a market in violation of laws, are duty unpaid and in noncompliance with regulatory measures. Illicit cigarettes can be genuine products manufactured by, or under ownership of a trademark owner and sold without payment of applicable taxes, or they can be counterfeit cigarettes.

Statistics show that 11.6 per cent of the global cigarette market is illicit, equivalent to 657 billion cigarettes a year and $40.5 billion in lost revenue. If the global illicit trade were eliminated, governments would gain at least $31 billion.

---

[3] J. Collin, E LeGresley, R MacKenzie, S Lawrence and K Lee, Complicity in contraband: British American Tobacco and cigarette smuggling in Asia Tobacco Control 2004; 13: 104-111

[4] http://www.theeuttingedgenews.comlindex.php?article=s 1427.

[5] http:lwww.medindia.netlnews/view_news_main.asp?str=1&x=15985.

Contraband Cigarettes in India

The quantum of contraband in India is perhaps to the tune of about 7000 crores annually which translates to a loss of about Rs. 2,500 crores to the exchequer as such products evade excise duty, import duty, octroi, corporate income tax and other taxes.

These smuggled cigarettes come through various routes such as:

(a) Mis-declared goods imported through air/sea.

(b) Cigarettes meant for duty free consumption routed to domestic market.

(c) Airline crew and passengers and professional carriers bringing the illicit cigarettes.

Smuggling of cigarettes is not in the exclusive domain of any one category but happens in all categories of cigarettes i.e. top, middle and low end. Brands which are more habitually smuggled into India are Marlboro, Benson and Hedges, 555, Next, More, Pine, Davidoff, Gudang Garam, Gold Leaf, Aziz Gold, etc. Some of the cigarettes in the low end category are Re. 1 cigarettes which are mainly smuggled from Bangladesh into India.

The tax component (Excise, Octroi, Entry tax, Corporate income tax, etc.) on cigarettes is about 60 per cent to 65 per cent of M.R.P. Since the smuggled cigarettes evade such a huge chunk, they are able to offer lucrative margins to the retail traders who are more than willing to stock and sell such products.

Spurious Medicines

Questions Answered By Bejon Misra (Founder-Consumer Online Foundation) regarding sale of spurious medicines.

1. What is the extent of counterfeiting in Pharmaceutical industry, as per official estimates and industry estimates.

This is an extremely difficult question to answer. In India there has been several studies conducted on this issue but none have till date has been able to convince the global community on the data existing as of today due to various reasons. The key reason is that manufacturing medicines in India is not effectively and efficiently regulated, even though medicines can not be manufactured without an official Government license and all medicines manufactured should go through regular inspections and testing by the State regulatory authority. However, in practice this is not enforced in the manner desired by us. The figures range from 0.04 per cent to 35 per cent are perceived as spurious in the sully chain of medicines in India. I would personally say it is not more than 1 per cent after looking into various existing documents and the results published by Government in a regular manner based on the test results of samples collected from the marketplace. PSM India has just concluded in drafting a methodology on a proposed study to be conducted in India jointly by all the stakeholders with support from Government of India and other organisations working on this issue globally.

2. Which are the areas where such medicines are sold.

The most sensitive or vulnerable points are rural locations and Government procurements for public hospitals. Even normal retail outlets are not free from spurious and sub standard medicines.

3. How effective is the mechanism to check standards of medicines produced including quality checking.

The existing system is not robust and needs to be designed scientifically to ensure well qualified persons who handle such sampling and testing procedures. All results on samples collected from various points for testing needs to be shared in public domain and action taken reports needs to be displayed for public scrutiny.

4. Has the industry identified the areas which are most affected by this problem.

Yes, the industry knows that the most vulnerable place is Government procurement policies, which encourages fly by night operators and are only based on bidding process irrespective of quality and efficacy of the medicines. The unauthorized manufacturers who do not adopt Good Manufacturing Practices are given license to manufacture medicines without physical verification of the manufacturing premises and the facilities/capacity of the manufacturing units for the purpose applied for grant of license.

5. What are the safeguards employed by Government agencies while procuring medicines for use in hospitals run by Government and local bodies.

All the procedures and processes are only on paper. None follow the prescribed certification procedure for procurement. There is practically no safeguards while procuring medicines and even if some organisations apply the process while procuring medicines, the storage and distribution system are extremely porous and ineffective in catching the culprit polluting the supply/distribution chain.

6. Is industry prepared to promote use of genetic drugs which are cheaper as compared to patent.

Yes, they are prepared provided Government encourages a level playing environment and brings strong regulatory mechanisms in the existing system. State Regulatory Bodies are under staffed and ill equipped to handle the enormous task to tackle the menace of spurious and sub standard medicines in India. The pharmaceutical industry in India are keen to support Sale of Generic Medicines to the extent possible and viable.

7. Use of technology to check menace of Counterfeit drugs.

This is the only solution available today. There are several successful technologies to detect and verify the authenticity of the medicines in the supply chain. The science of tracing and tracking the medicines from the manufacturing point to the end user can be mapped easily. Several responsible Pharmaceutical Industries are already adopting the technologies to protect their brands and the market share.

COUNTERFEITING IN ALCOHOLIC BEVERAGES

Questions answered by Mr. Pramod Krishna, Director General, CIABC

1. What is the extent of counterfeiting in Alcoholic beverages industry, as per official estimates and industry estimates.

8%-10%

2. Which are the areas where such stocks are sold.

Where duties are high between states on border areas.

3. How effective is the mechanism to check standards of beverages produced including quality checking.

State Excise is responsible but good companies keep a quality check in house.

4. Has the industry identified the areas which are most affected by this problem.

As above.

5. What are the safeguards employed by Government agencies like defence while procuring beverages for use by Defence forces.

Quality checks.

6. Use of technology to check menace of Counterfeit beverages.

Holograms, Bandrolls < Barcodes, Guala Caps.

Chapter 6

Counterfeiting and Piracy Pose Danger for Consumers

A recent study conducted by Business Action to Stop Counterfeiting and Piracy indicates that the global value of counterfeit and pirated goods, currently $650 billion, is likely to more than double by 2015. In recent years, the range of counterfeit goods has expanded significantly and no industry has been spared. While damage to rights holders may be obvious, consumers can be just as seriously affected, as counterfeit goods may cause physical illness, injury or even death. Unsurprisingly, the US Federal Bureau of Investigation has named counterfeiting 'the crime of the 21st century'.

According to Rahul Sethi, a partner at Ranjan Narula Associates, and a member of the International Trademark Association's Anti-counterfeiting Committee, India is not new to counterfeiting. In 2005, the European Union reported that India was the world's largest supplier of fake drugs, responsible for 75 per cent of counterfeit medicines globally. About 38 per cent of medicines supplied in government hospitals in India are said to be counterfeit, and 40 per cent of all drugs sold in Indian markets spurious. Those involved include not only organised crime syndicates, rogue pharmaceutical companies, corrupt local and national officials and terrorist organisations, but also medical professionals, such as pharmacists and physicians.

A bane of poor countries in particular, manufacture, distribution and storage of counterfeit drugs and medicines are not always known and are seldom reported. The production of counterfeit pharmaceuticals can be as simple as producing alternative packaging materials using a laser printer or as complicated as the production of the original product.

In India, the manufacturers can be loosely grouped into three categories: unlicensed manufacturers who operate out of small cottage factories, licensed manufacturers who secretly make fake drugs alongside their legitimate products, and importers who bring in drugs from China and then fraudulently repackage them.

Counterfeiters may produce licensed pharmaceuticals by day and knock-offs by night. One case in point involved a pharmaceutical company in Gurgaon, Haryana. When the Food and Drug Administration confronted the owner with evidence of the counterfeit goods, he disavowed all knowledge of the products except for one: a tablet containing a new generation antibiotic ciprofloxacin. Upon testing at the state and central drug laboratories, it was found that the pill contained no ciprofloxacin at all, and the company's manufacturing license was revoked.

District drugs control officer, Rakesh Dahiya, said that though they had been picking up different drug samples from the manufacturer, Chem Pharma, it was the first time their samples failed in the mandatory tests. "We had some preliminary reports indicating that the manufacturer was involved in making fake drugs. Finally, when we received the confirmed report, we picked up samples of Cipro Floxacin and found that the absence of some salts from the antibiotic made it of no use to the patients," Dahiya added.

As far as pharmaceuticals are concerned, Dr. Naresh Gupta of Maulana Azad Medical College, says, "For the poorest consumers, the choice may be between questionable medicine and no medicine at all. The ultimate solution to this dilemma is ensure that they are never forced to make this choice, and that life-saving medication is available to all. Until this is possible, vigorous law enforcement is essential to protect the most vulnerable of consumers."

However, it isn't all bad news. Recently, the World Health Organisation (WHO) has put in place a mechanism to define counterfeit medical products. The set of definitions of substandard, spurious, falsely labelled, falsified and counterfeit products will be globally accepted and help to bring about uniformity in identifying such drugs, without interrupting worldwide supplies.

Carrying the same harmful potential, albeit on a relatively modest scale, are the spurious rubber products, like the "O" rubber rings used in domestic pressure cookers. A similar enterprise can be found engaged in the manufacture of adulterated cosmetics.

In India, a market where Unilever is the largest fast moving consumer goods (FMCG) player, there are over 113 look-alike of its leading fairness cream, Fair and Lovely, available. Vicks, Axe, Ariel, Parachute, Johnson's Baby Powder, Clinic Plus, Dove, Lux, Colgate, Pears, Fair and lovely, Coldarin are just a few of the brands that are affected by pass-offs and counterfeits. Pass-offs are lookalike products that resemble the original products, mainly through misspelling of the trademark. For example, Sunslik instead of Sunsilk, Clemic Plus or Climic Plus or Cosmic Plus instead of Clinic Plus, Collegiate for Colgate, Vips Rub or Vives Rub as a pass-off for Vicks Vaporub.

A Procter and Gamble official says that the company is engaged in various initiatives to train its sales force and field staff to create awareness on the problem and also initiate action at the point of sale where counterfeits and pass-offs are available. Last year, industry chamber FICCI had set up an anti-smuggling and counterfeit committee to provide knowledge support to the industry in understanding and tackling counterfeit, contraband

and smuggled products. Price differences among neighbouring countries, tax arbitrage and ineffective control are a few reasons for illicit trade."Domestic duty evaded goods by small, fly-by-night manufacturers without obtaining the stipulated licence from central authorities is the modus operandi for smuggled goods," the chamber said.

The devil in the lack of authenticity is also present in textile manufacture. It seems nothing escapes the hawk-eye scrutiny of counterfeiters when they think of how to prosper in their nefarious trade. Considering that the imitated version of a high-priced item would fetch more money than the spurious variety of a low-priced one, the counterfeiters are very resourceful in making them.

Globalization is regarded by some people as giving rise to counterfeit products. With a view to cut costs and to increase production, reputed manufacturers outsource their production processes elsewhere with lower standards of labour laws and environmental regulations. Such local producers see no reason to stick to the standards after meeting their commitments and flood the markets with shoddy replicas of reputed brands.

This is very true of some consumer items, especially very expensive or desirable brands as also of merchandise that are easy to reproduce cheaply. Such manufacturers of spurious goods either attempt to deceive the consumer into thinking they are purchasing a legitimate item, or convince the consumer that they could deceive others with the imitation.

Recently, the Comite Colbert (a non-profit conglomerate of 70 luxury companies representing more than 130 professions in ten categories: haute couture and fashion design, perfume, gold and jewellery, silver and bronze, leather, crystal, faience and porcelain, champagne, fine wine and cognac, hospitality and gastronomy, publishing and decoration) launched an aggressive new anti-counterfeiting campaign.

FICCI has also said that illicit trade in cigarettes in India is one of the highest in the world. High excise duty on cigarettes has resulted in the growth of contraband trade of the product with the total market estimated to reach Rs 1,900 crore in 2012, up nearly 12 per cent from the previous year, according to industry estimates. In 2010-11, the size of contraband cigarettes market in India was around Rs 1,700 crore. According to industry players, 17 billion cigarette sticks are smuggled into the country every year, making India the sixth highest consumer of smuggled cigarettes in the world. "Smuggled and contraband cigarettes are becoming a bigger and bigger problem in India. There are lot of illegal cigarettes, which are smuggled from outside India and even counterfeit products are also sold in huge quantity," an official working with a cigarettes company said. When asked about the factors behind the increase in illegal trade of the product, he said, "Extreme high excise duty and VAT rate on cigarettes in India make smuggling a particularly attractive proportion."

Counterfeit goods and pirated software and optical media also continue to thrive in India. A report by the United States Trade Representative (USTR) has named Nehru Place and Palika Bazaar in New Delhi, Richie Street and Burma Bazaar in Chennai, Manish Market, Heera Panna, Lamington Road and Fort District in Mumbai, and Chandni Chowk in Kolkata as markets that need to be watched out for this high-volume trade. Piracy and counterfeiting, including counterfeiting of medicines, remains widespread and India's enforcement regime remains ineffective at addressing this problem. Amendments are needed to bring India's copyright law in line with international standards, including and implementing the provisions of the WIPO Internet Treaties. Additionally, a law designed to address unauthorised manufacturing and distribution of optical discs remains in a draft form and should be enacted in the near term," the report said.

Though Rahul Sethi feels that India has a robust legal framework for combating counterfeiting and piracy, he feels that there is still much to be done in the area of enforcement. "The establishment of dedicated enforcement cells, trained in handling IP matters, and fast-track specialized IP courts would greatly improve the system."

According to the Havocscope Global Black Market Index, the market value of counterfeit and pirated goods in India is:
- Books: $38 million
- Auto parts: $1.15 billion
- Movies: $959 million
- Music: $17.7 million
- Software: $2739 million
- Games: $129.9 million

Orchie Bandyopadhyay

CHAPTER 7

Public Awareness—Sword against Counterfeiting and Smuggling

In the recent past, India's economic growth story has attracted world's attention, which has brought a new set of challenges for the domestic economy. A few of these are counterfeits, pass-offs and smuggling that are threatening domestic brands and industry. The rapid advancement in information, communication and technology is further boosting the growth of such illicit activities. International studies indicate that by 2015, the total impact of the trade in counterfeits and pirated goods, including the value of domestically sold fakes, those traded on the internet and the added costs to society through lost taxes and jobs—will exceed $US1 trillion dollars. All this is (1) Hurting the integrity of the brand thus eroding sales of the legitimate product; (2) Undermining local industry, Discouraging legal imports; and (3) Reducing volume of revenue collection from duties and levies by the State. It also means less public funding for services such as health, education and social welfare. Further, INTERPOL in particular have also noted the continuing increase in the distribution and consumption of products which are highly dangerous to human health and safety and the United Nations inter-regional Crime and Justice Research institute have reported the specific involvement of major international organized criminal gangs in the trade in fakes.

Tarnishing Brand India

In 2005, the European Union reported that India was the world's largest supplier of fake drugs, responsible for 75 per cent of counterfeit medicines globally. About 38 per cent of medicines supplied in government hospitals in India are said to be counterfeit, and 40 per cent of all drugs sold in Indian markets spurious. Those involved include not only organized crime syndicates, rogue pharmaceutical companies, corrupt local and national officials and terrorist organizations, but also medical professionals, such as pharmacists and physicians. Global marketing research firm AC Nielsen has reported that 10 per cent to 30 per cent of cosmetics, toiletries and packaged goods in India are counterfeit. The Automotive Component Manufacturers Association of India estimated that the annual value of fake spare parts is around Rs. 87 billion (approximately $2 billion) in a sector worth Rs. 248 billion (approximately $5 billion). An international survey conducted by ICC- Business Action to Stop Counterfeiting and Piracy (BASCAP) puts BRAND INDIA amongst nations with an unfavorable IP environment. This, in a way reinforces poor perceptions about the Indian landscape, and puts us closely behind China and Russia. The menace of smuggling and counterfeiting is affecting not only individual brands but BRAND INDIA. Most business decisions related to product development, manufacturing investment, technology transfer, setting up new ventures and procurement are influenced by the IP environment of a country. The present state of affairs has an indirect impact on the FDI being attracted to India. While India has fared well on revamping its IP legislation it has lagged behind on other critical parameters such as effective enforcement resources; public education and its understanding of IP rights; public awareness and its cooperation with enforcement.

Legal Framework in India

India has no legislation dealing specifically with counterfeiting and piracy, but statutory, civil, criminal and administrative remedies do exist in various statutes, including:

- the Trademarks Act 1999,
- the Copyright Act 1957,
- the Patents Act 1970,
- the Designs Act,
- the Geographical Indications Act 1999,
- the Drugs and Cosmetics Act 1940
- the Prevention of Food Adulteration Act 1954,
- the Consumer Protection Act 1986,
- the Indian Penal Code, the IT Act 2000, and
- the Customs Act 1962.

India has a robust legal framework for combating counterfeiting and piracy; its laws in this regard are among the best in the world. However, there is still much to be done in the area of pulling up infrastructure for enforcement. The establishment of dedicated enforcement cells, trained in handling IP matters, and fast-track specialized IP courts would greatly improve the system. The Indian Government is making steady progress in this area through establishment of State Judicial Academies and Conducting Capacity building programs for judicial, customs and police officers.

FICCI CASCADE and Public Awareness on Counterfeiting and Smuggling

The Federation of Indian Chamber of Commerce and Industry (FICCI) with this backdrop took the initiative to launch the Committee on Anti-Smuggling and Counterfeiting Activities Destroying the Economy (CASCADE) on 18 January 2011 at FICCI Federation House, New Delhi with overwhelming response from the industry. The Committee has multi-pronged approach. It aims at

- Generating awareness on the hazardous impact of smuggled, contraband and counterfeit products on Consumers and Citizens
- Capacity building of law enforcement agencies including Judicial, Police and Customs Officers
- Research and propose law reforms for effective enforcement of IP related laws.
- Systematic dissemination of enforcement techniques, procedure and strategy through regular workshops for the guidance of its members.

FICCI CASCADE has recently launched a consumer/public education and awareness campaign on the effects of counterfeit and smuggled goods on the economy in India. The campaign specifically aims to highlight health and safety risks, especially in the case of counterfeit medicines, toys, cosmetics, food, beverages, auto and airplane parts; network and data security in case of counterfeit software and audio-visual products, besides the impact on jobs, tax revenues and abetment to criminal economy that counterfeits and smuggled goods provide. In the first phase it has launched a joint publicity campaign with the Ministry of Consumer Affairs under their *Jago Graahak Jago* campaign in February 2012. FICCI CASCADE is further initiating another wave of sensitization on the issue. This campaign would be in collaboration with Delhi Government's "BHAGIDARI" initiative. With the partnership with Delhi Government's *Bhagidari* Campaign, FICCI CASCADE aims to heighten the seriousness of the hazards of smuggled and counterfeit goods in the minds of an average consumer and motivate every citizen to be a "CASCADER."

Forging ahead with its mission FICCI CASCADE believes that it is important to bring the youth on board the awareness campaign and through them influence the society as a whole about the serious threat posed by smuggling and counterfeiting.

To achieve this FICCI CASCADE has joined hands with a national Level NGO in the 5th Hum Kishore Festival from 30 April to 4 May 2012. The festival theme this year will be "Fight Smuggling and Counterfeiting." Over ten thousand students belonging to various schools in the NCR will participate in this joint campaign in the form of Hum Kishore Festival. This Festival encouraged youth to be socially responsible citizens. It is further envisaged that the message would trickle down to family units through our youth, the leaders of tomorrow. FICCI CASCADE remains committed to forge ahead consistently working on these critical factors to take BRAND INDIA forward.

A Note on Illegal Cigarettes

With the levy of VAT on Cigarettes in 2007 and the unprecedented increase in Excise Duty in 2008, which was in the order of 140 per cent and 390 per cent on regular and micro size non filter cigarettes respectively, the legitimate cigarette industry was forced to substantially vacate these categories. This created a large vacuum at a convenient and affordable price, and stimulated a large scale entry for tax evaded filter cigarettes. These illegal duty evaded filter cigarettes, which are sold at a price point of Rs. 1 per

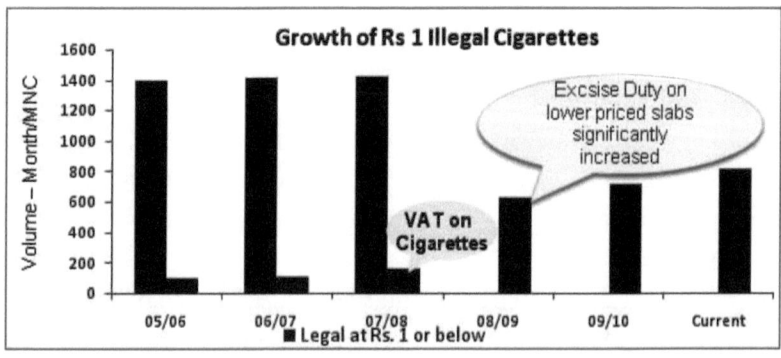

stick, do not even cover the cost of taxes (Excise Duty of Rs.998 per thousand cigarettes plus VAT, Entry Tax or other Local Taxes as may be applicable). It is estimated that such illegal filter cigarettes account for 10 per cent of the Indian market, resulting in an estimated revenue loss of Rs. 1,200 crore annually.

As per the Euromonitor International, a well respected research organization, total illegal cigarettes (i.e. domestic duty evaded and smuggled) in India account for 16 per cent of the industry, having grown by 58 per cent between 2004 and 2009. India is now the 6th largest illicit cigarette market in the world.

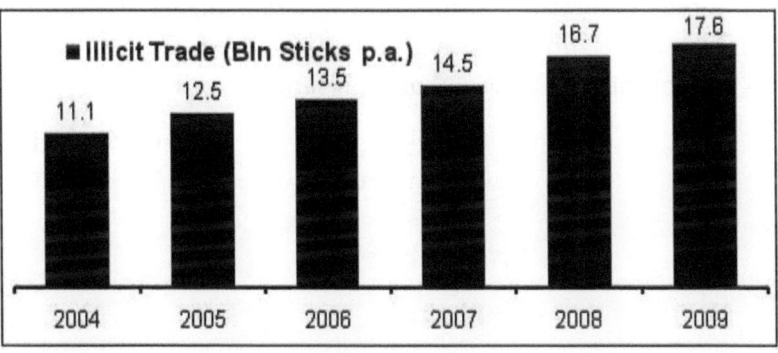

The problem has been exaggerated due to arbitrary hike in VAT and other State Taxes on Cigarettes which has afforded an attractive arbitrage opportunity for smuggling and illegal inter-State movement of stocks.

This menace of cigarette smuggling, due to disparity in rates of tax, has also been acknowledged by the Task Force on Indirect Taxes headed by Dr. Vijay Kelkar, in the following words:

"As regards tobacco products, it has been the experience of many countries that differential taxes on such high-excise goods particularly cigarettes, invites large scale illegal cross-border movement resulting in huge evasion of revenue.... Unregulated tax rates on such high value goods have also been seen to lead to displacement of domestic tax-paid cigarettes by contraband products, translating to significant losses in revenue."

The illegal trade of Cigarettes not only deprives the Industry from legitimate share of profit and the Revenue from the corresponding share, but it also encourages the entry of organized criminal syndicates, which could have serious consequences concerning law and order. Internationally it has been reported that illegal profits from cigarette smuggling have been used to fund terrorist activities.

Recognizing the catalytic impact of high duty rates on smuggling, countries like Bulgaria and Ireland have refrained from any increase in tax rates in a bid to combat smuggling Per annum, per capita Cigarette consumption is much higher in Bulgaria (2150) and Ireland (950) than India (99). Even Canada lowered tax rates on cigarettes to combat smuggling from USA.

Meenu Chandra,
Head CASCADE Division, Joint Director, FICCI

CHAPTER 8

Contraband Cigarettes Big Business

To complicate matters it has been observed that when on the rare occasion the Excise or Custom department manage to confiscate such smuggled cigarettes these are again released into the market through public auction but without mandatory markings (such as Statutory Warning, MRP, Date of Manufacture, etc.). Therefore, it is indirectly the Government itself which is facilitating transgression of the Law.

DUTY UNPAID CIGARETTES (ILLEGAL MANUFACTURER)

It is impossible to sell cigarettes at such low prices as they sometimes are, as the duty component is more than the price at which they are sold. Needless to say, the unscrupulous manufacturers of these cheap quality cigarettes are evading payment of taxes/duties. Due to such gross evasion of duty, very high margins of commission can be accorded to the wholesalers and retailers of such illegal products. This in turn results in the stockists/retailers aggressively selling such cheap brands to consumers, including teenagers and minors who are price-sensitive consumers.

In fact many dealers pass these cheap duty unpaid cigarettes (which have catchy English/foreign names as imported cigarette brands) which young persons and minors are attracted to. The consumption of such brands has tremendously spurted, as these cigarettes are available at a very cheap price. This is especially true of young persons who find such cheap cigarettes extremely attractive and affordable to buy. It has been observed that after the wide-spread availability of such cigarettes consumption amongst teenagers and minors has increased particularly in rural areas and among lower section of the society.

REGULATIONS

International regulations and treaties assert a stance which is against illicit trade in any form.

The Parliamentary Committee Report on the Cigarettes and Other Tobacco Products Bill, 2001 which was a Parliamentary Committee constituted with 43 members and headed by veteran politician, Shri S. B. Chawan, has also cognised for the major problems that have been created by smuggled cigarettes.

Similarly, the Report on Tobacco Control in India published by Ministry of Health and Family Welfare, Government of India has gone into the problems caused by smuggling and its deleterious effect on tax policy.

(a) As per Cigarettes Act, 1975, Section 2(m), 3 and 4(2) the Statutory Warning is made compulsory. In fact Section 3(3) makes the Statutory Warning compulsory even for imported cigarettes.

Similarly, the Cigarettes and Other Tobacco Products Act, 2003 under Sections 3(o), 7 and 8 mandate that Statutory Warning is compulsory on all tobacco products including imported tobacco products [Section 7(3)].

As smuggled cigarettes either do not have the Indian Statutory Warning or have Warnings in alien languages (such as Russian, Japanese, Chinese, Thai, Bengali, etc.) the Warning is not communicated and consumers get an impression that such cigarettes are safe/safer.

(b) Under Rule 6 of the Packaged Commodity Rules under the Standards of Weights and Measures Law every packet of cigarettes must contain the following mandatory declaration:

(a) Date of Manufacture / Packing.
(b) Maximum Retail Price.
(c) Name and Address of the Manufacturer.

However, smuggled cigarettes do not contain these mandated markings.

Obviously, the stipulation that packaged commodity must contain the name and address of the manufacturer and the month and year in which the commodity is manufactured has been brought in by the Parliament with the prime purpose of informing the consumer that:

- the goods are manufactured by the particular manufacturer.
- that the goods are not old stocks or dated. This is even more important because cigarettes are ingested/consumed by citizens and therefore these stipulations must be strictly followed.

(c) Under the Consumer Protection Legislation the Statement of Object and Reasons of the Consumer Protection Act, 1986 clearly stipulates that the Act is to promote and protect the right of consumers such as:

- the right to be protected against marketing of goods which are hazardous to life and property.
- the right to be informed about the quality, quantity, potency, purity, standard and price of goods to protect the consumer against the unfair trade practices.
- the right to be assured that consumers' interest will receive due consideration at appropriate forum.

The protection of the consumers is a mandated aspect of law which is completely made impossible by the rampant presence of smuggled cigarettes in the market.

Anil Rajput
Chairman, FICCI-CASCADE and Senior Vice President
–Corporate Affairs, ITC Ltd)

CHAPTER 9

Introduction to Counterfeiting and its Impact on Automotive Sector

COUNTERFEIT IN GENERAL

A counterfeit is an imitation, usually one which is made with the intent of fraudulently passing it off as genuine. Counterfeiting exists in the forgeries of currency and documents, as well as the imitations of clothing, software, pharmaceuticals, watches, electronics, auto components and company logos and brands. Product counterfeiting is usually by nature an organized group activity, because the manufacture of goods in a holistic way requires manpower as well as time, and the goal is usually that of profit. Many jurisdictions take the offence quite seriously and product counterfeiting can be considered as organized crime under the respective national law.

Counterfeiting in the automotive sector is not a new phenomenon and dates back to the 1980s when counterfeiting first became a visible threat to automotive component businesses. As a result of the sophisticated global economy, coupled with easy access to technological advances, very few product lines are able to escape the reach of counterfeiters. Re-engineering products or duplicating labels, packaging and logos is becoming increasingly easy with speed, accuracy and relative anonymity.

GLOBAL AUTO COMPONENTS SCENARIO

The following are some intriguing global facts on counterfeits:

- According to a report by the Federal Trade Commission (FTC), counterfeiting is estimated to cost the global automotive parts industry US$12 billion per annum in lost sales; of this total, US$3 billion is in the US.
- It is also estimated that lost sales in the auto parts industry in the US correlates to potentially 200,000–250,000 fewer manufacturing jobs.
- More than 80% of goods seized at US borders are produced in China.
- An estimated 30% of products sold in mainland China are counterfeit.
- A 2006 Frost and Sullivan report is not optimistic about the future, which is reflected in its projection of losses as high as US$44.7 billion to the global auto industry by 2011.

In the automotive components sector, various auto components in the aftermarket are counterfeited on a massive scale. Products such as filters, spark plugs and brake pads, bearings, piston and piston rings etc. tend to be more prone to counterfeiting than others. Below is a list of the most commonly counterfeited automotive parts.

Most Commonly Counterfeited Parts

Engine and exhaust	Suspension and braking	Body and Structural	Electrical/electronics
Oil filters	Steering arms	Sheet metals	Alternators spares
Air filters	Tie rods	Bumpers	Head lamps
Distributor caps	Brakes	Windshields	Tail lamps
Fuel filters	Brake linings		Wipers
Coolant and transmission fluids			Starter motor spares
Bearings			
Oil pumps			
Water pumps			
Spark plugs			
Piston and piston rings			
Lubricants			
Sealing rings			

As the Indian automotive market is growing exponentially, the issue of counterfeiting in auto components is already assuming serious proportions. This white paper is an attempt to investigate counterfeiting in auto components and highlight the issues and adverse impact to the government and to society at large.

Counterfeiting of Auto Parts in India

Overview of the Indian Auto Sector

The Indian automotive industry occupies a prominent place in the Indian economy. Due to its deep forward and backward linkages with several key segments of the economy, the automotive industry has a strong multiplier effect and acts as one of the most critical drivers of economic growth. The industry has witnessed unprecedented growth in recent years, owing chiefly to the increasing affluence of the average consumer, overall gross domestic product (GDP) growth, the arrival of ultralow-cost cars and the increasing maturity of Indian original equipment manufacturers (OEMs).

The well-developed Indian automotive industry ably fulfills its economic and social role by producing a wide variety of vehicles: passenger vehicles, two-wheelers, three-wheelers and commercial vehicles. Passenger vehicles accounted for a 17.4 per cent share of the total automobiles produced in India in 2009–10.

The Indian automotive industry reached a size of US$ 36 billion in 2009–10, and is estimated to reach US$ 155 billion by 2016. The overall production increased from 8.4 million in 2004–05 to 14 million vehicles in 2009–2010, while overall vehicle sales (including domestic sales and exports) increased from 8.5 million units to 14 million units in the same period.

The sector witnessed an upsurge in the shift of manufacturing plants and units of global car manufacturers such as Honda, Volkswagen, Mercedes and Ford, etc., from overseas to India due to India's inherent low-cost advantage, healthy domestic demand and the availability of skilled labor workforce.

The total automotive exports from India increased from 0.63 million vehicles in 2004–05 to 1.8 million vehicles in 2009–10. The primary driver of this growth was the cost advantage due to factors such as low labor costs and increased emphasis on quality.

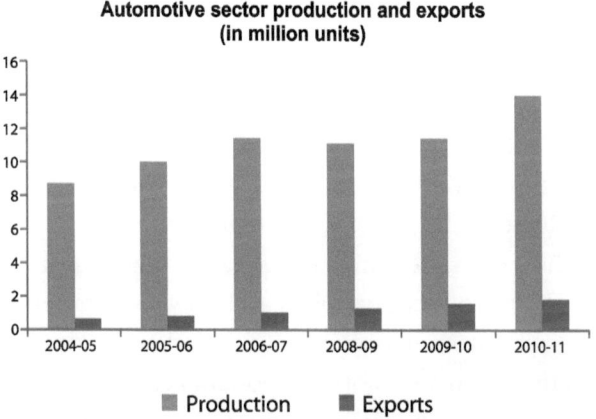

India is expected to witness strong growth in vehicle production till 2020 across all segments.

Passenger vehicles - projected to be 5 million units by 2015 and over 9 million by 2020 driven by domestic demand and as a global hub for exports of small cars.

Commercial vehicles – volumes of over 1.4 million by 2015 and over 2.2 million by 2020. Small Commercial Vehicles (SCV), a relatively new segment, expected to grow 28 per cent annually over the next few years.

Two and three wheelers – expected to double to 22 million units by 2015 and reach 30 million by 2020 driven by low penetration levels, expanding rural sales and growth in exports.

Tractors – projected to be over 0.7 million by 2015 and over 1 million by 2020 with steady growth expected in **domestic and export volumes.**

Construction equipment – likely to grow 2.5 times to 0.1 million units by 2015 and almost double to 0.18 million by 2020 driven by investments in the infrastructure sector.

Achievement of these production volumes will position India as one of the top 5 vehicle producing countries in the world.

Overview of The Indian Auto Components Sector

The automotive components sector in India has grown at a tremendous pace during the last decade. The industry size is estimated at INR 990 billion (US$ 22 billion) in FY10, and over the five-year period between FY05 and FY10, the industry's production increased at a CAGR of 20 per cent.

Over the years, leading India-based manufacturers have diversified their product portfolios and now cater to a number of segments of the automotive component market. During FY10, the engine and drive transmission components contributed to half of the total auto components in production in the country.

Auto Components: production trend

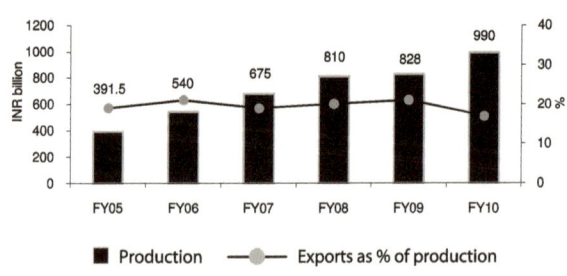

Source: ACMA

Based on end-user segments, original equipment manufacturers (OEMs) accounted for 75 per cent of the total domestic auto components consumption in FY10. The OEM segment is relatively safe from counterfeits, as the products are directly supplied to vehicle manufacturers.

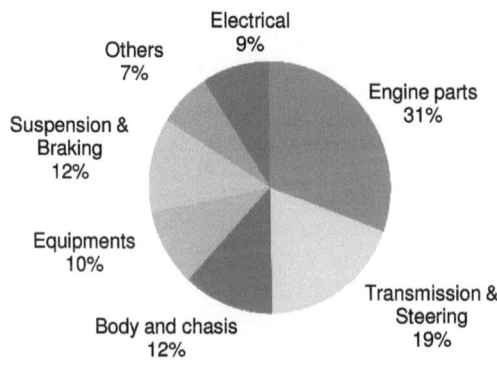

Auto Components: production-wise composition of production (FY10)

- Electrical 9%
- Others 7%
- Suspension & Braking 12%
- Equipments 10%
- Body and chasis 12%
- Transmission & Steering 19%
- Engine parts 31%

Source: ACMA, Ernst & Young estimates

However, counterfeit components severely impact the aftermarket, which accounts for approximately 25 per cent of the total consumption. The size of aftermarket for auto components in India is estimated to be INR 247.5 billion in 2010, increasing from INR 160 billion in 2004.

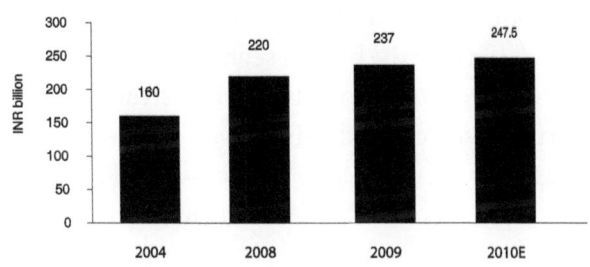

Size of Aftermarket Auto Components (in INR billion)

Year	INR billion
2004	160
2008	220
2009	237
2010E	247.5

Source: ACMA, Ernst & Young estimates

After excluding estimate for counterfeit, the aftermarket segment can be further divided into OEM branded parts (both as OE spares and for independent after market), OE (tier-1) suppliers, independent manufacturers, imports and counterfeit parts (including grey imports). The OEMs account for 34 per cent of the aftermarket, OE suppliers account for 30 per cent and independent manufacturers' account for 23%.[1]

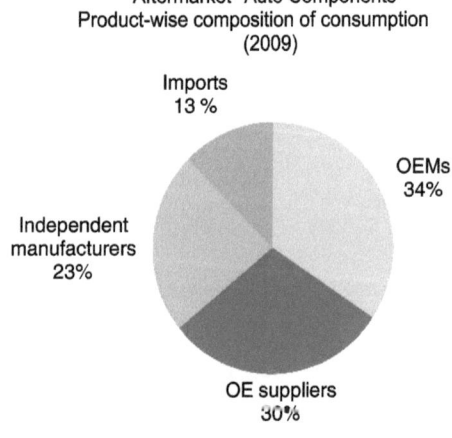

Source: Ernst & Young estimates

In terms of product-wise composition of aftermarket, engine and exhaust related parts are the biggest segment accounting for 24 per cent of the total consumption. Body and structural parts, and electrical parts are second and third largest segments with 22 per cent and 21 per cent share respectively.
In terms of product-wise composition of aftermarket, engine and exhaust related parts are the biggest segment accounting for 24 per cent of the total consumption. Body and structural parts, and electrical parts are second and third largest segments with 22 per cent and 21 per cent share respectively. The automotive components sector currently faces a number of challenges

---

[1]This pie excludes counterfeit parts that are estimated to account for 35 per cent of the aftermarket.

including capacity constraints, threat from low-cost manufacturing countries etc.

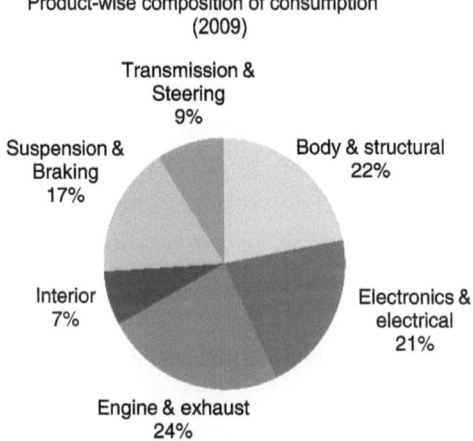

Source: Ernst & Young estimates

Introduction to Counterfeiting of Auto Parts in India

However, a much larger challenge at hand is arising from a growing number of spurious manufacturers engaged in the manufacture/assembly of counterfeit automotive components.

The sudden increase of such counterfeit components in the sector has impacted the genuine parts market in the country. This is a visible threat to the industry, and a combination of measures are needed to curb this menace.

Supply Chain of Automotive Components

In a genuine automotive component supply chain, the manufacturer of auto components sources raw material either domestically or from an international supplier.

The manufacturer can be the OEMs or independent (tier-I) manufacturers of auto parts. Vehicle manufacturers receive their supply of components from Tier I suppliers.

The manufacturer then supplies the part to its distributors who in turn services the aftermarket. There may be a regional distributor in the aftermarket supplying the component to sub-distributors, or there may just be regional distributors for the product.

The part is supplied from distributors to retailers or directly to large workshops. Finally, the component is sold to end consumers either directly or by replacing the part in their vehicle in the course of maintenance or break down service. This supply chain is generic and may not apply to all types of auto components, and some may have a very straight forward or even more complex supply chain.

Genuine Automotive Parts' Distribution Channel

Supply Chain for Spurious Auto Components

Counterfeit auto components are manufactured locally and also imported from out side India.

Local manufacturing: Parts that do not require high-end manufacturing technology and substantial investments are manufactured on the outskirts of metro cities such as New Delhi and Mumbai.

Imported parts: Parts that require modern machinery and

significant investment are generally imported from low-cost countries such as China, Thailand and Indonesia.

These products enter the supply chain after they are packaged, either in fake packaging or in original packaging sourced from mechanics or service stations) and then sold to a master distributor.

The distributors can usually be found in major markets such as Opera House in Mumbai and Kashmere Gate in New Delhi. Sometimes, small brokers are deployed to get the products into the supply chain. Relatively small players without big set-ups, brokers function as suppliers for certain products and take them from importers, manufacturers or distributors to the aftermarket.

These products are mostly sold as fake ones until they reach the wholesale market, but at the retailer level, they are sold as either original or "locally produced" goods. The term fake is generally not used in the market.

Factors Impacting Counterfeiting

Counterfeiters take advantage of the lacunae in the system to take their products to market. Lack of strict laws and the absence of stringent punishments for offenders have resulted in the counterfeit business gaining size. Packaging units in various parts of the city manufacture duplicate packs and spurious products are then packed and shipped to different markets. These packaging units have seldom faced any crackdown from authorities in many years.

Various factors can be held responsible for the increase of counterfeiting of auto parts in India. Based on primary research input from various distributors, dealers, mechanics and service station, the study has identified the following as the primary factors that drive the counterfeiting activity in the market.

Counterfeit Automotive Parts Distribution Channel

[Flowchart showing counterfeit automotive parts distribution channel with boxes for: OEM (Vehicle manufacturer, OEM Dealer); Raw material or component (Domestic supplier, International supplier, Unauthorized International/domestic supplier); Auto component manufacturer (Domestic manufacturer, Distributor, Unauthorized manufacturer/packaging company); Master distributor/importer; Broker; Aftermarket (Service centers/workshops, Retailer); End user]

Manufacturing

Based on our field work, we have come to the conclusion that some products are being easily manufactured in India. The required raw materials and technology are easy to acquire hands-on and, hence, local sourcing and manufacturing is gaining popularity among counterfeit suppliers across the country. For example, automotive filters are being locally manufactured in the Burari area on the outskirts of New Delhi. These filters are then shipped to wholesale markets, where a master distributor or broker makes a deal. They are then supplied to retailers and workshops via a range of channels. Delhi-based manufacturers also produce other counterfeit parts. Other than tier-I cities, small cities such as Ludhiana in Punjab are emerging as important locations for the manufacture of counterfeit mechanical auto components.

Packaging

Our study findings indicate that genuine spares are sold to local mechanics and workshops without their outer packaging. Further, this packaging is used for selling counterfeit products, which generally come without their outer packaging. At times, for parts of Indian OEMs vehicles, the packaging material of counterfeit components is also manufactured locally. These spares are sold with genuine packaging and counterfeit products and marketed to customers as genuine products.

Importing: The supply chain of counterfeit auto components also varies between car manufacturers. For instance, the supply chain of counterfeit components of European car manufacturers differs from that of Indian car manufacturers. According to market intelligence, wholesalers source counterfeit products through importers or aggregators based in Mumbai and New Delhi. Importers source counterfeit components from the following countries:

Part	Country
Spark plugs	China, Korea
Diesel filter inserts	China
Lighting systems	China
Piston rings	Taiwan
Clutch plates	Taiwan, China
Alternators	China
Fuel pumps	Taiwan, China
Gear box assembly	China, Taiwan
Brake shoe	China
Bearings	China

However, we believe that local manufacture constitutes a chunk of spurious supply of components and that imports have a smaller yet significant share.

Higher margins: Findings from our study indicate that the margins earned by selling counterfeit parts of Indian cars are usually 35 per cent–50 per cent, while for others, this can go up to 55 per cent–75 per cent. Hence, the relatively low margin on genuine products along with a highly competitive environment at the dealer level is becoming an important factor driving the sales of counterfeit parts.

Push factor (retailers and mechanics): Due to relatively high margins and the ease of sourcing, retailers and mechanics are increasingly pushing to sell a counterfeit product rather than a genuine product, even when they have a genuine product in stock. Our findings also indicate that false guarantees are often provided for such counterfeit products.

Pull factor (uninformed customers): As India is not a top-end vehicles market, price-sensitive and uninformed customers tend to look for cheap replacement parts while getting their vehicles serviced or repaired. Customers such as owners of vehicles older than 5-7 years, taxis and fleet operators (non-owner driven vehicles) try to get the job done at a relatively low cost. Our findings indicate that this leads to excessive bargaining and, hence, promotes the sale of a counterfeit over a genuine part.

Short replacement cycle: Findings from our study indicate that majority of parts that are counterfeited on a large scale have a short replacement cycle. For some components such as suspension parts and brake pads, this can be attributed to lack of good infrastructure such as paved and smooth roads. Hence, there is a tendency to opt for cheaper substitutes and not for genuine parts each time a replacement is needed.

Supply Constraints: Lack of availability of genuine parts for older variants of vehicles, and sometimes even for new models, is serving as a driver for counterfeit sales. This may either be a supply constraint at the manufacturer's end or it a strategy at the distributor level to achieve high margins, by citing less availability as a reason. Our findings indicate that master distributors sometimes create an artificial supply shortage to get high margins.

SHORTCOMINGS OF EXISTING LEGISLATIONS

Our survey brings out clearly that according to the aftermarket industry players, the existing laws do not address adequately the menace of business in spurious auto components adequately in addition to not providing the required deterrent commensurate with the gravity of the offences. The agencies that carry out anti-counterfeiting actions including raids, initiation of criminal proceedings etc., also confirm these limitations.

Secondly, there is a strong belief that the present laws do not mandate action by the state of its own accord. This is borne out also by the survey wherein members are of the overwhelming view that the state should assume pro active role to monitor, survey and book the offenders engaged in the business of spurious auto components.

The second part of this report addresses the legal aspects of dealing with the menace, the current legislations, its limitations and the refinements in law recommended for dealing with the problem more effectively.

Replacement counterfeits: A few uninformed customers also demand imported counterfeits as they perceive these counterfeits to be safe and unlikely to cause any major concern. However, they are unaware of the harm some of these counterfeits could cause to their vehicles' life, increase fuel consumption and also pollute the environment due to higher emission of pollutants. According to our findings, the imported components are manufactured in Mexico or East European countries and supplied to India via Dubai.

Chinese Impact

The China effect: The unprecedented growth of Chinese manufacturing has been one of the key drivers of the twenty first-century global economy. Much of this growth is the result of outsourcing by overseas companies looking to take advantage of China's high productivity and low costs. Most of the retail value of these products accrues to companies doing the outsourcing, while Chinese manufacturing firms retain a relatively small share. This mutually beneficial arrangement is only possible because most Chinese firms respect the intellectual property (IP) rights of outsourcing companies.

Unfortunately, this situation, in which designers and manufacturers of a product often live on different continents, has fostered the growth of counterfeiting. Counterfeiting is an attractive alternative to legal commerce because costs are reduced to manufacturing, transport and distribution, and the costs involved in research, design and marketing are all avoided. In China, counterfeiters are essentially unaccountable so they have no interest in building a brand reputation. They are able to reduce costs by cutting corners in the production phase, such as employing sweatshop labor, engaging in environmentally unsound manufacturing processes and using inferior-grade materials. This has become a modern-day phenomenon in China and other low-cost manufacturing countries.

China, along with Taiwan, accounted for more than 65 per cent of the total counterfeit goods (including automotive components) seized at the European Union border in 2008. Other major countries of origin include the UAE, Turkey and Indonesia.

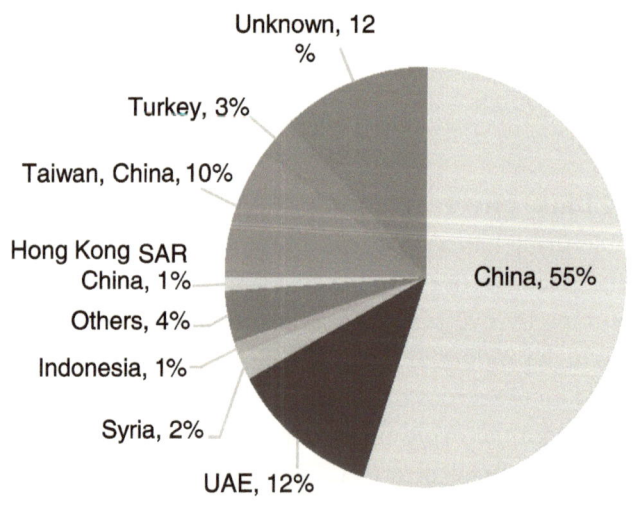

Origin of Counterfeit Goods Seized at the European Customs Union Border, 2008

Source: United Nations Office on Drugs and Crime (UNODC)

India's Auto Component Imports from China

Between 2006 and 2009, India's automotive component imports from China grew at a CAGR of 30 per cent and the figure crossed US$1 billion in 2008. Auto component imports from China contribute more than 20 per cent of the total imports in India (US$ 938 million, INR 42 billion); it is difficult to arrive at a figure of counterfeit imports from China, but as previously mentioned, some statistics indicate that imports from China may be contributing a great deal to the counterfeit market (around 80 per cent of the goods seized in the US are manufactured in China).

Also, a number of Chinese parts suppliers have an online presence on sourcing websites such as Alibaba.com. After taking a closer look at the products these suppliers are selling, we conclude that they are using product codes of OEM suppliers to advertise their products and, hence, it can be said that a significant number of parts that are being imported from China for aftermarket consumption are counterfeits. These may come packaged as original parts from China, or they may be packaged locally in India.

Impact of Counterfeiting

Counterfeit automotive components result in various kinds of losses, which pertain to loss of revenue for the government and for genuine-part manufacturers and also the loss of lives in fatal road accidents. Counterfeits can also result in the loss of jobs, extra fuel consumption in vehicles and the loss of brand image for manufacturers. Based on our research, we have tried to quantify the variety of effects of counterfeits.

Size of the Counterfeit Market in India

Our findings suggest that counterfeit automotive components account for approximately 35 per cent of the aftermarket, which is estimated to be around INR 247.5 billion (US$5.5 billion). Given that the scale of the problem is enormous, the losses and other effects are also considerably large.

Impact on the Government and the Economy

Loss of Government Tax Revenue

As counterfeit activity is not subject to any fiscal imposts, government loss is the additional tax revenue that the government may have earned if these parts were produced by genuine manufacturers. We estimate that the government is losing close to INR 22 billion (US$496 million) per annum due to the sales of counterfeit automotive components.

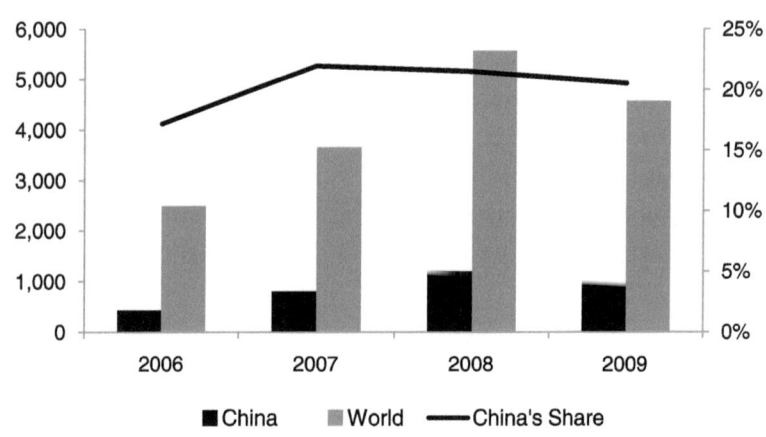

Import of Auto Components in India and Share of China in Total Imports (US$ million, %)

■ China ■ World —— China's Share

Source: International Trade Center

Loss of Government Tax Revenue

FY10	Value
Total market for auto components	INR 990 billion (US$ 22 billion)
Share of aftermarket	25%
Value of aftermarket	INR 247.5 billion (US$ 5.5 billion)
Share of counterfeit components	35%
Value of counterfeits	INR 87 billion (US$ 1.9 billion)
Excise duty	10%
Other taxes	15%
Loss to government*	INR 22 billion (US$ 496 million)

Source: ACMA, Ernst and Young research.
*Indicative figure—calculated by assuming an average tax rate and profit margin on these automotive components.

Job Losses

The automotive component sector provides direct as well as indirect employment to more than 8 million people in India. The figure for additional jobs that the sector is estimated to generate in the absence of counterfeiting can be taken as jobs lost due to counterfeiting. According to our estimates, this figure currently stands at more than 1.15 million jobs. This is a large number even for a populous country such as India.

Impact on the End-users and Others

Road Accidents in India

With sales of vehicles growing over the last two decades, the incidence of road accidents in India has also increased. According to latest official data from the National Crime Records Bureau, road accidents were responsible for more than 35 per cent of total accidental deaths in the country in 2009. Moreover, in 2009, casualties in road accidents increased by 7 per cent.

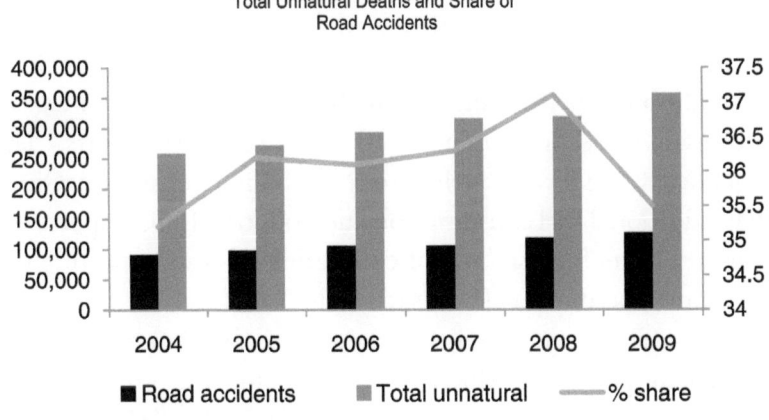

Total Unnatural Deaths and Share of Road Accidents

Source: National Crime Records Bureau (India)

Commercial vehicles such as trucks and buses account for around one-third of all road accident deaths in the country, with two-wheelers accounting for around 21 per cent and cars for around 9 per cent. Two-wheeler deaths can be attributed to the fact that they are unsafe to drive due to offering less protection as compared to a fully covered vehicle. However, in the case of heavy commercial vehicles and cars, the use of counterfeit parts is also a potential cause The primary reason behind this is the short replacement cycle of parts (such as brake pads) and low levels of customer awareness. Another factor could be the willingness of fleet operators and drivers to buy spurious products at less expensive prices. Hence, this increases the risk of accident leading to even fatal accidents.

Based on primary research inputs, we estimate that around 20 per cent of total road accidents in India can be either directly or indirectly attributed to the use of counterfeit automotive parts. The use of counterfeits resulted in around 25,400 deaths and more than 93,000 injuries during 2009.

Additional Fuel Consumption and Pollution

One of the many disadvantages of using counterfeit parts is the additional fuel consumed due to their usage. According to our estimates, the end-users are consuming close to 109 million liters of additional petrol and approximately 8 million liters of additional diesel is attributable to use of counterfeit parts.[2] The monetary value for this is close to INR6 billion per annum. Given that Additional fuel consumption and pollution India imports the majority of its fuel, the use of counterfeits is also impacting the government as more fuel needs to be imported.

It has also been noted that the use of counterfeits results in additional pollution which is harmful for the environment. Driving an average polluting light vehicle for 15,000 kilometers

---

[2]This has been calculated by taking the vehicle part in the country and calculating the number of vehicles that are prone to counterfeit parts that impact fuel consumption. The average mileage of these vehicles has then been taken to reach an estimate for additional fuel consumed.

per year, equivalent to 160g/km of carbon emissions, will result in the release of 2.6 tonnes of carbon dioxide (CO_2) into the atmosphere. For a vehicle that is using counterfeit auto parts, this figure is estimated to increase by around 10-15 per cent. Further, the corresponding figure for heavy commercial vehicles is even higher. This additional pollution not only hampers the environment, but also results in various health problems. Hence, the government expenditure to tackle diseases caused due to pollution also increases with the increased use of counterfeit auto parts.

INCREASED DOWN TIME OF THE VEHICLE AND HIGH COST OF REPAIRS DUE TO FREQUENT FAILURE

Another major consequence of using counterfeit parts is that they lead to frequent vehicle break-down and high cost of repair. This cost is incurred by the end-user who buys counterfeits instead of genuine parts either knowingly or unknowingly. If all the additional costs (fuel, break-down, repair etc.) incurred by using counterfeits are factored-in in the price, the use of a counterfeit part turns out to be a lot more expensive than buying a genuine part.

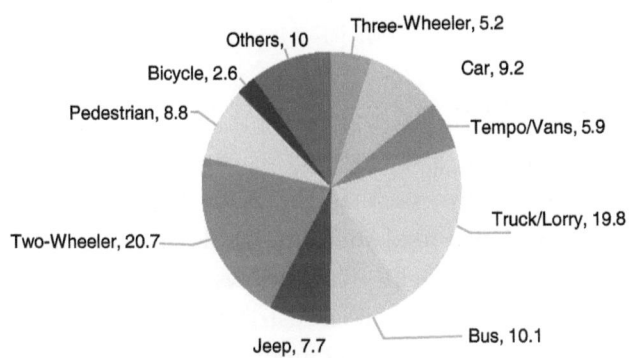

Road-Accident Deaths by type of Vehicle (% share, 2009)

Source: National Crime Records Bureau (India)

Actions Taken by Component Manufacturers and ACMA

Automotive component manufacturers and ACMA have been working together to wipe out the counterfeiting of automotive components. Their collective initiatives can be classified into two buckets:

Conducting raids/seizures

Many of the ACMA member companies are regularly conducting their own raids to protect their brand across the country. Huge quantities of spurious auto parts are seized regularly during these raids.

Under the umbrella of ACMA, member companies have also started conducting common raids across the country by hiring specialized agencies. Mentioned below are some key statistics on common raids conducted by ACMA and its members:

- A total of 128 raids were conducted in 2009.
- As many as 311 raids were conducted in 2010.
- Members are targeting 500 raids across various cities in 2011.
- Thousands of fake and spurious components have been seized in the past one year.
- Members have spent millions of rupees in setting up specialized teams and conducting raids and seizures in the last few years.

Spreading awareness

ACMA members are also conducting shows titled Asli-Nakli during industry events such as the Auto Expo, Partmart and Autocare etc. And also road shows in wholesale markets such as Kashmere Gate in New Delhi. These shows are aimed at educating retailers or wholesalers as well as customers about the impact of these counterfeit automotive components. These shows have attracted a great deal of participation. The members plan to conduct 90 such shows in 2011, with 30 shows in North India and 20 shows each in East, West and South India.

Awareness program for the ACMA member companies

For the benefit of member companies, ACMA conducts awareness program. ACMA also provides training to its members on intellectual property rights, copyrights, trademarks, design, patents etc.

These help the members to know their rights to protect their brand. The first awareness program was conducted for the southern members of ACMA during Dec'10 to be followed in other regions during 2011.

PRIMARY SURVEY RESULTS

Ernst and Young conducted a primary survey of automotive component players to get viewpoints on the counterfeiting menace. These players include suppliers of various types of automotive parts to all segments of the industry (PV, CV, two-/three-wheeler etc.). The sample also has a mix of companies that supply to OEM's and the aftermarket. Following are some of the key observations that emerged from the results.

Viewpoints on the counterfeiting of automotive components

More than 55 per cent of the respondents of the survey believed that their company is impacted by counterfeit automotive parts. This is an alarming number, considering that the survey had the participation of a mix of OEM and aftermarket suppliers. This indicates that the business of the majority of aftermarket suppliers is impacted by counterfeiting in India.

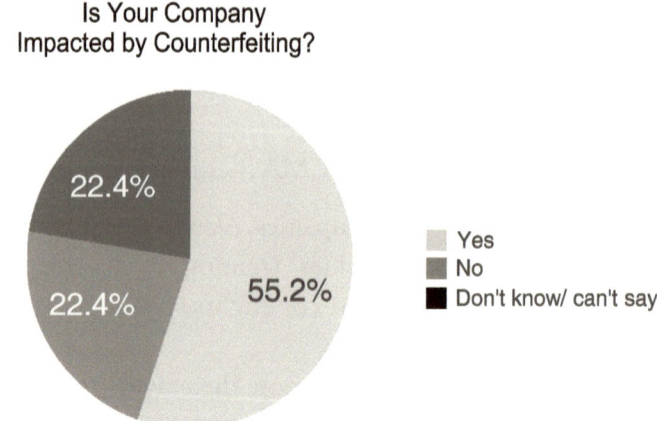

In our study, we attempted to assess the impact of counterfeits on the manufacturer's total revenue. Around 32 per cent of the respondents estimate the loss to be less than 10 per cent, but at the other end of the spectrum, 25 per cent respondents believe that the loss was greater than 30 per cent.

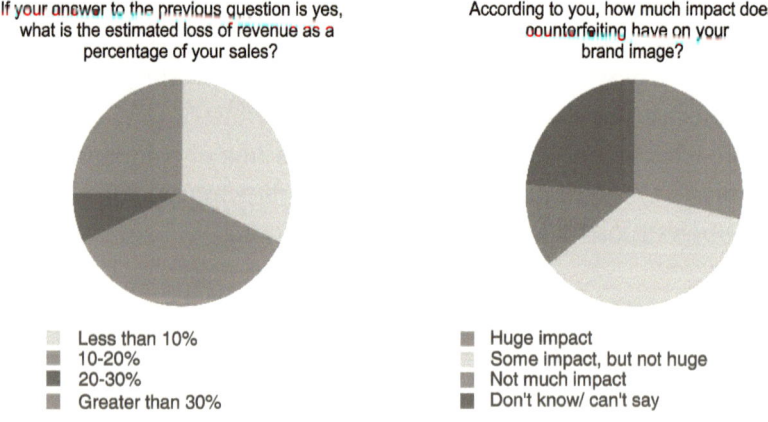

According to the respondents, diesel filters and spark plugs are most prone to counterfeiting. The top five products also include clutch plates, lighting systems and shock absorbers. The replacement cycle for all these products is quick, and they are also readily available at local shops.

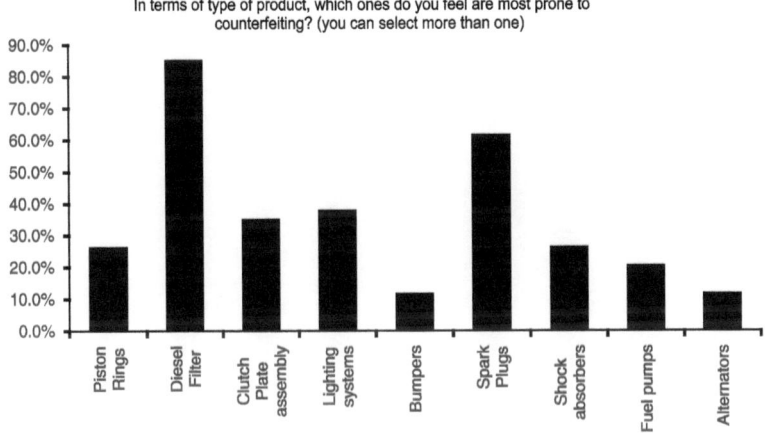

Around 64 per cent of the respondents to the survey believe that counterfeiting has a damaging effect on their brand image. Of these, around 29 per cent believe that it has a "huge impact." This figure confirms the concern of aftermarket automotive components suppliers that it is not only monetary loss but also the loss of brand image that is damaging for the industry.

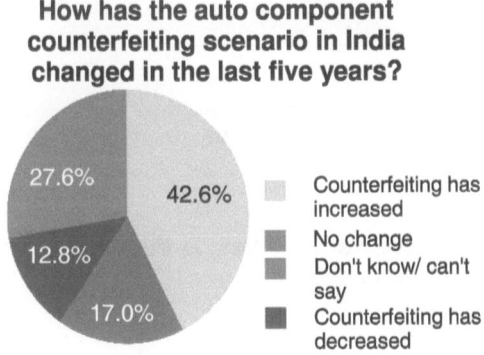

Most of the respondents (43 per cent) believe that counterfeiting has either increased in the last five years or has remained at the same level (17 per cent). However, the staggering majority (around 60 per cent) believe that counterfeiting is set to grow in the next five years. This is quite a disconcerting statistic, specifically as it comes from people present in the aftermarket.

Do you expect counterfeiting to grow in the next five years?

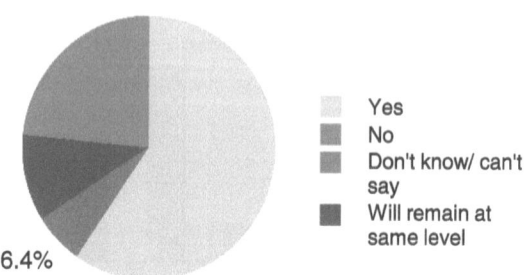

- Yes
- No
- Don't know/ can't say
- Will remain at same level

6.4%

When asked about counterfeits of their company's products, about half of the respondents have come across the same in the market. Around 39 per cent believe that the product is illegally packaged locally, and around 57 per cent felt that the product is imported from low-cost countries such as China.

Have you come across an imported counterfeit for your product?

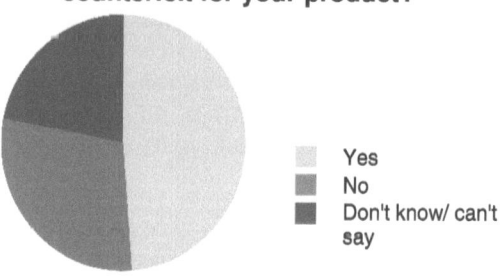

- Yes
- No
- Don't know/ can't say

If the answer to is yes, is the product packaged locally?

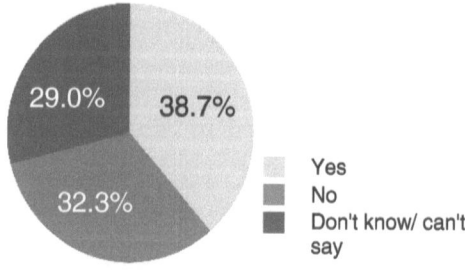

29.0%   38.7%
   32.3%

- Yes
- No
- Don't know/ can't say

If the answer to above is yes, do you believe that it is imported from China or a similar country?

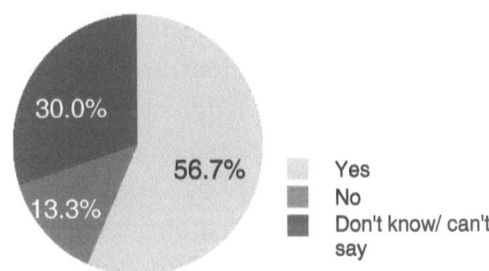

We have also tried to gauge, through our survey, the factors that impact the counterfeiting of automotive components. As already mentioned in the report, the margins that dealers enjoy on counterfeit products are far higher than their original counterparts.

According to the results of our survey, almost half the respondents believe that the margins enjoyed by selling counterfeits exceed 30 per cent. This evidently includes all the taxes that would have been paid to the government if the products were subject to fiscal imposts.

In your opinion, what are the average margins enjoyed by dealers by selling counterfeit products?

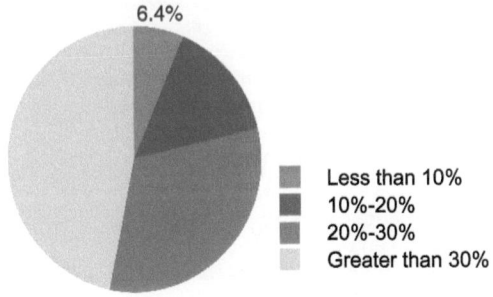

On the factors responsible for the growth of counterfeiting, most of the respondents believe that lack of strict action against culprits is the primary factor. This is followed by lack of awareness on the counterfeit product on the part of the dealer and the customer and the harm it can possibly cause. Low margins on genuine parts and lack of safety regulations for aftermarket components were ranked third and fourth, respectively.

When asked about what is required to restrain the act of counterfeiting, most of the respondents believed that more stringent laws were the need of the hour. Spreading consumer and dealer awareness, regular raids and curbing less expensive imports were ranked second, third and fourth, respectively.

The majority (56 per cent) of the respondents believe that the government should initiate action against the spurious automotive component industry. Furthermore, an overwhelming number of respondents (78 per cent) favor stricter laws to help curb counterfeiting in this sector.

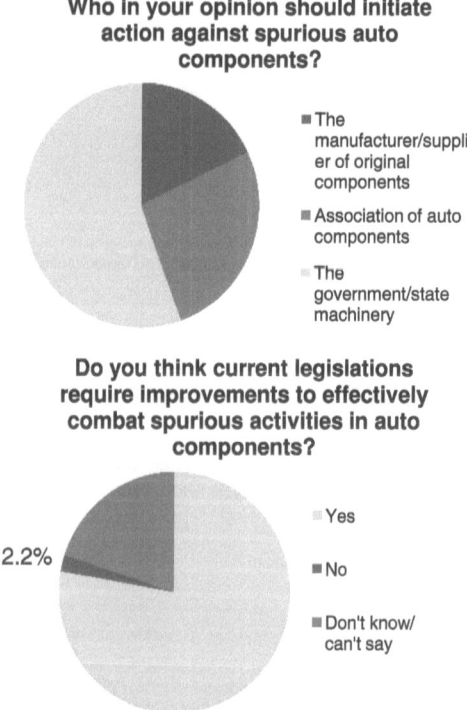

Profile of the respondents

The respondents to our survey were automotive component manufacturers based in India. These include OEM suppliers and those who supply both to OEMs and to the aftermarket.

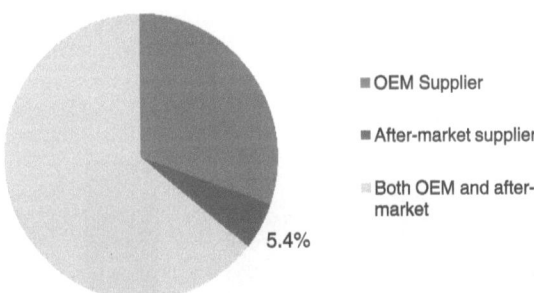

What best describes the nature of business of your company?

- OEM Supplier
- After-market supplier
- Both OEM and after-market

5.4%

Directors, C-level executives and/or a part of the senior management of representative organizations constituted the majority of the respondents.

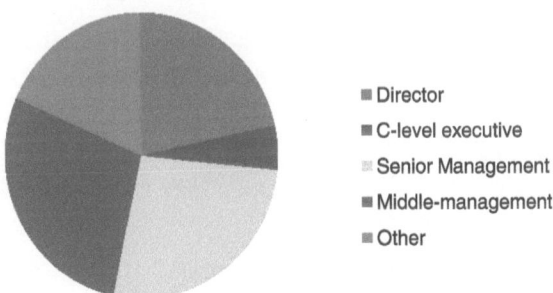

What best defines your role or function?

- Director
- C-level executive
- Senior Management
- Middle-management
- Other

The respondent set also covers a large number of components such as engine parts, chassis and drive transmission. They also cater to a wide variety of vehicle types, including passenger vehicles, commercial vehicles and two- or three-wheelers.

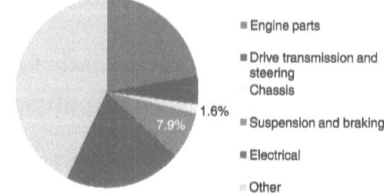
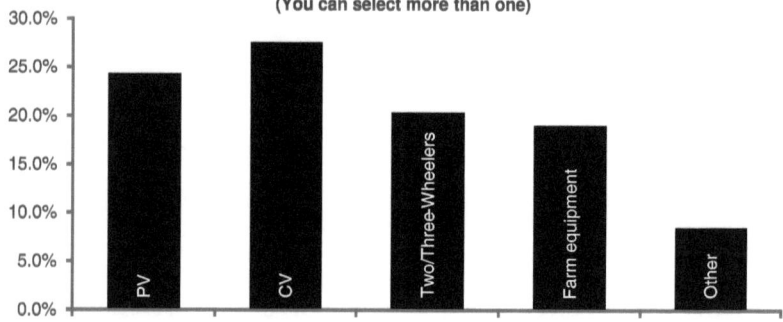

Among the participants, around 30 per cent have a turnover of more than INR10 billion and over 40 per cent have a turnover of INR1–10 billion. The remaining (around 28 per cent) have a turnover of less than INR1 billion.

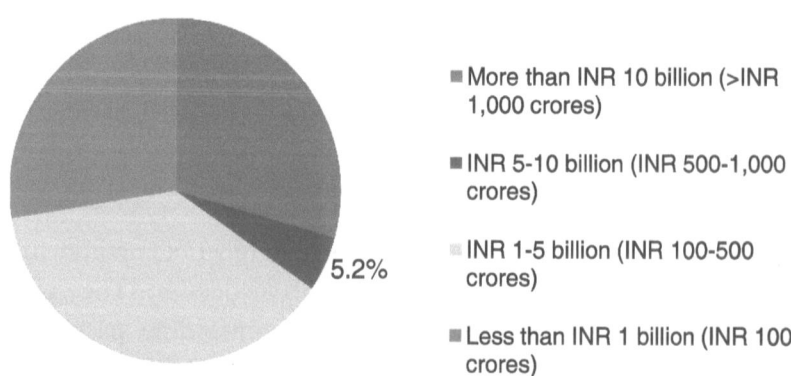

Legal Issues and Legislative Aspects

Legal Definition of Counterfeit or Spurious Auto Component

A fake or spurious auto component has to pass the test in law of what constitutes "counterfeit". Counterfeit is an imitation of the original part which is replicated and marketed as original with intent to deceive the customer into believing that the part is original coming from a business house of repute. Use of well known brands or deceptively similar or look alike brands, design or other intellectual property of another, packaging, presentation, color scheme and sub-standard quality of the component are the usual ingredients of a fake auto component.

The expression "counterfeit" is, defined under Penal Code to mean an act of causing one thing to resemble another thing intending thereby to practice deception or knowing it to be likely that deception will thereby be practiced. Identical imitation is not essential to counterfeiting (Explanation I). The legal presumption is that the counterfeiter intends to practice deception until the contrary is proved (Explanation II).

As per the Consumer Protection Act, 'Spurious Goods' means 'goods' which are claimed to be genuine but are actually not so and manufacture of spurious goods or offering such goods for sale is an unfair trade practice for which complaint is maintainable.

If we adopt the definition of spurious product under the Drugs and Cosmetics act, mutatis mutandis, 'spurious auto component' would mean imitations or attempt to pass off as genuine, components which are sold with the incorrect or fictitious name of the manufacturer or the product.

For the purpose of effectively dealing with the menace, it is very essential that counterfeit or spurious auto components are defined in a comprehensive way preferably under the Motor Vehicles Act.

Automotive Parts and After Market Parts

The automotive aftermarket is seriously impacted by spurious automotive components. The United States Automotive Parts Industry Annual Assessment 2009 refers to automotive parts as either 'Original Equipment' (OE), or 'Aftermarket' parts. Original equipment parts are used in the assembly of a new motor vehicle (automobile, light truck, or truck) or are purchased by the manufacturer for its service network referred to as Original Equipment Service (OES) parts. Suppliers of OE parts are broken into three levels. The first level is "Tier 1" suppliers who sell finished components directly to the vehicle manufacturer. The next level is "Tier 2" suppliers who sell parts and materials for the finished components to the Tier 1 suppliers. Third level is "Tier 3" suppliers who supply raw materials to any of the above suppliers or to the vehicle assemblers directly.

Aftermarket parts are divided into two categories: replacement parts and accessories.

Replacement parts are automotive parts built or manufactured to replace OE parts that become worn out or damaged. Accessories are parts made for comfort, convenience, performance, safety, or customization and are designed for add-on after the original sale of the motor vehicle.

This white paper addresses the issues concerning "Automotive Parts (excluding Accessories) which are spurious or fake or counterfeit, the three expressions being used interchangeably. A fake or spurious auto component is very likely to be sub-standard but a substandard auto component may not be fake or spurious.

Overview of Existing Legal Remedies (of Significance to Auto Component Industry)

The focus of this white paper is to propose legislative refinements to specifically address the issue of fake or spurious auto components. This paper will not be complete unless we take a critical look at the dispensation by the existing enactments, their applicability and adequacy and shortcoming in combating the menace of spurious auto components on a national canvas and by way of an institutionalized approach.

Contact Act 1872

This oldest and time tested piece of legislation gives relief in case of breach of contract. Breach of Contract gives right of action to the aggrieved party i.e. if the product supplied is not in conformity with the contract. For relief under the Contract Act, privity of contract between the contracting parties is essential. It cannot effectively deal with product liability claims of third parties arising out of defective product. Suffice to say that in the context of a supply of fake or spurious auto component, this law bestows on the customer a right of action depending upon whether the breach is a breach of a condition or of a warranty, the earlier breach gives right to repudiate the contract and the later one gives right to claim damages.

The Contract Act gives relief to the contracting parties, but does not and is not intended to serve as a deterrent law to check the manufacture, storage or packing of fake or spurious products and is much less intended to safeguard the interest of the general public or consumers at large except when an offer is made to public at large.

Sales of Goods Act

The sale of Goods Act addresses the rights and duties of parties to the Contract and the process of concluding the sale, consequences of breach etc.

The Sale of Goods Act does not address compensation for damage to person and property caused by a defect in the product.

Essential of Commodities Act, 1955

Section 3 of the Act enables the Central Government if it is Overview of Existing Legal Remedies (of significance to Auto Component Industry) of the opinion that is necessary or expedient so to do for maintaining or increasing supplies of any essential commodity or for securing their equitable distribution and availability at fair prices, it may by order, provide for regulating or prohibiting the production, supply and distribution thereof and trade and commerce therein. Prior to omission of clause (a) of Section 2 of the Act, vide The Essential Commodities (Amendment) Act 2006 (54 of 2006) with effect from 12.02.2007, "essential commodity" did include "components, parts and accessories of automobiles."

Under the Act, any person who contravenes any order made under section 3 shall be punishable with imprisonment for a term varying between three months and seven years and fine. As per Section 11 of the Act, notwithstanding anything contained in the Code of Criminal Procedure, 1973, every offence punishable under the act shall be cognizable and non-bailable. Section 12A of the Act mandates that offenses relating to certain products such as foodstuffs, edible oilseeds and oil, drugs etc (including "components, parts and accessories of automobiles" up to 12.02.2007) shall be tried in a summary manner by a Judicial Magistrate of the first class empowered on that behalf by the State Government or by a Metropolitan Magistrate.

The provisions of the Essential Commodities Act affords a good basis for legislating that offenses in connection with manufacture, packing, sale, stocking and distribution of spurious auto components will be considered as cognizable and non-bailable and also for trying such offenses in a summary way. This requires appropriate provision preferably in the Motor Vehicles Act that concerns automotive industry/products.

Consumer Protection Act 1986

Section 2 (f) of the Act defines "defect" as any default, imperfection or shortcoming in the quality, quantity, potency, purity or standard which is required to be maintained by or under any law for the time being in force or under any contract, express or implied, or as is claimed by the trader in any manner whatsoever in relation to any goods.

As per Section 2 (j) of the Act, "manufacturer" means a person who makes or manufactures any goods or part thereof or does not make or manufacture but assembles parts made or manufactured by others or puts or causes to be put his own mark on any goods made or manufactured by any other manufacturer.

As per Section 2 (oo) of the Act, "Spurious Goods" means such goods which are claimed to be genuine but they are actually not so.

As per Section 2 ® "Unfair Trade Practice" means a trade practice which for the purpose of promoting sale, use or supply of any goods adopts any unfair method or unfair practice or deceptive practice including inter-alia, the practice relating to :

- False representation that the goods are of a particular standard, quality, grade, composition, style or model;
- False representation that any rebuilt, second hand, renovated, reconditioned or old goods as new goods;
- Representation that the goods have sponsorship, approval, performance, characteristics, accessories, uses or benefits which such goods do not have;
- Makes to the Public a materially misleading representation purporting a warranty or guarantee of a product or goods;
- Permits the sale or supply of goods intended to be used or likely to be used by consumers knowing or having reason to believe that the goods do not comply with the standards prescribed by competent authority relating to performance, composition, contents, design, construction, finishing or packaging as are

necessary to prevent or reduce the risk of injury to the person using the goods;

- Manufacture of spurious goods or offering such goods for sale.

Redressal of Consumer Disputes

Chapter III of the Act provides for a three tier redressal mechanism by District Forum, State Commission and National Commission (the later two agencies having appellate jurisdiction) based on value of goods in respect of which complaint is made and the amount of compensation, if any claimed. The reliefs awarded by the agencies are essentially civil in nature including pecuniary compensation. However if the complainant fails to comply with the order of the redressal agencies, he shall be punishable with imprisonment for a term which shall be not less than one month but which may extend to three years or with fine or with both.

A serious limitation of The Consumer Protection Act is that relief is available only to a consumer as defined under this Act. A person who obtains the goods for resale or for any commercial purpose is outside the scope of the Act. Secondly the punitive provisions though intended to compensate the aggrieved complainant, is not sufficient enough to be a deterrent against the unscrupulous supplier of spurious goods.

The redeeming feature of the Act is that it affords a comprehensive definition of manufacturer, defect, spurious goods, unfair practice etc. These can form a good basis for inclusion of same or similar expressions in any legislation intended to combat manufacture, packaging, sale, stocking and distribution of spurious auto components without limiting its focus only on the ultimate consumer so that any stake holder could initiate remedial or punitive action for such offences.

Standards of Weights and Measures Act, 1976

Many of the automotive components are offered for sale in packaged form. In this context it is relevant to know that this Act prescribes certain discipline on the manufacturer, packer or seller of the packaged commodity. Chapter IV, Section 39 of the Act provides that no person shall make, manufacture, pack, sell or cause to be packed or sold or distribute or deliver or cause to be delivered or offer, expose or possess for sale any commodity in packaged form to which Chapter IV applies, unless such package bears thereon a definite, plain and conspicuous declaration made in the prescribed manner of:

• The identity of the commodity in the package,

• The net quantity in terms of standard unit of weight or measure,

• The accurate number, if it is sold by number,

• Unit sales price etc.

Penalty for the contravention of Section 39 can range up to a fine of Rs. 5,000 for first offence and for the second and subsequent offence with imprisonment for a term which may extend up to five years and also with fine.

Within the given mandate of this law, the Standards of Weights and Measures Act, 1976 and the Packaged Commodities Rules 1977 is a fine example of the state taking upon itself the responsibility to protect the Consumer. Although it is a piece of central legislation, the state has the concurrent authority to make its own law and is also responsible for administering this legislation.

This piece of legislation recognizes the need to protect consumer interest with the state taking the lead in a pro active way. *The Legal Metrology law (The Weights and Measures Act and the Rules and the Packaged Commodities Order) provide a reliable analogy for according to and for the state to assume a 'suo motu' role for monitoring and punishing offences in connection with manufacture, packaging, sale, stocking and distribution of spurious auto components.*

Patents Act

A patent right is granted to an invention (usually of commercial importance) concerning technology used in relation to an article of manufacture or a manufacturing process. A spurious auto component may entail (but not always) infringement of a registered patent giving rise to the owner of the patent a right of action against the infringer of the patent. Any one indulging in the manufacture, use, sale, distribution, import etc of an automotive component purporting to infringe a registered patent can be held liable for such infringement. The burden of proof such infringement is usually on the owner of the patent or the licensee of the patent.

In a suit for infringement of patent, the courts award one or more of the following reliefs:

- Injunction restraining the infringer from use of the patented knowhow or process or manufacture of the patented product as the case may be.
- Damages or account profits.
- Seizure, confiscation and or destruction of the product as well as any material, machinery or dyes used in the manufacture of the product.

The limitation of Patent Act is that it does not mandate the patent authorities to initiate 'suo motto' action against infringement. It is for the owner or licensor of the patent to approach the appropriate court i.e., the district court or the High Court based on the pecuniary authority and within whose jurisdiction the cause of action has arisen.

Patent law is not in the nature of a surveillance law intended to bring within its radar all instances of infringement. Furthermore, the law does not impose criminal punishment on the infringer. Also, since all cases of spurious or fake products may not involve infringement of patent, this law is not a comprehensive remedy against spurious products.

Copyright Act

Copyright is inherent and automatic upon the creation of a work which is eligible for grant of copy right.

A manufacturer of an automotive component has a copy right as original owner in the engineering drawings, artwork and color schemes used in cartoons, product literature, service manuals, packaging, visual and audio creations, computer programs etc.

Registration of copyright is not compulsory but the certificate by the Registering authorities is a prima facie evidence of copy right in a dispute before a court of law.

Both civil and criminal action can be taken for infringement of Copyright. Civil remedies include injunction, damages, account profit etc. Administrative reliefs include confiscation of infringing material by excise authorities, restriction on import of products bearing infringing copyright material etc. As per First Schedule table II of the Code of Criminal Procedure, 1973, copyright infringement is a cognizable non- bailable offence punishable with imprisonment for a term varying between six months and three years and in the case of second or subsequent offence the minimum imprisonment term is one year which can go up to three years. The offence is also punishable with fine varying between Rs.50,000 and Rs. 2,00,000.

A police officer not below the rank of a sub inspector is authorized to seize without a warrant material infringing copyright. While the state machinery can initiate action based on information of copyright infringement without a formal complaint by any person, in actual practice the state machinery initiates action based on a complaint by the complainant.

The Copyright Act recognizes that it is as much the concern of the state to punish copyright offenders as that of the owner of copy right. This forms a good basis for recommending a 'suo motto' action by the state for booking those engaged in manufacture, sale, storing and distribution of fake or spurious auto components whether or not the offence violates a Copyright protection.

Trade Marks Act 1999

Chapter XII of the Act deals with offences and penalties. It sets out as to what constitutes application of trade mark, falsifying and falsely applying trade mark, penalty for applying false trade marks, trade descriptions, etc., penalty for selling goods or providing services to which false trade mark or false trade description is applied, enhanced penalty on second or subsequent conviction etc. Punishment for offences include imprisonment for a term not less than six months but which may extend to three years and with fine which shall not be less than Rupees 50,000 but which may extend to Rupees 200,000. Offence relating to false representation of a trade mark as Trade Marks Act 1999 registered is punishable with imprisonment for a term which may extend to three years or with fine or both.

The manufacture, marketing, distributing, packing and storing of spurious automotive components is more serious an offence than falsifying or falsely applying a trade mark and deserves severe punishment by way of imprisonment and or significant fine.

Designs Act

Under the Designs Act 2000, during the existence of any Copyright in a design, it is unlawful for any person to:

- For the purpose of sale, to apply or cause to be applied to any article or in any class of articles in which the design is registered, the design or any fraudulent or obvious imitation thereof, except with the license or written consent of the registered proprietor of copyright in that design;
- To import for the purposes of sale, without the consent of the registered proprietor, any article belonging to the class in which the design has been registered and having applied to it the design or any fraudulent or obvious imitation thereof;
- To publish or expose or cause to be published or exposed for sale an article knowing that the design or any fraudulent or

obvious imitation thereof has been applied to article in any class of articles in which the design is registered, without the consent of the proprietor.

Anyone who contravenes the above provisions of the Act is liable for every contravention:

- To pay to the registered proprietor of the design a sum not exceeding Rupees twenty five thousand recoverable as a contract debt or;
- If the proprietor elects to bring a suit for recovery of damages for any such contravention, and for injunction against repetition thereof, to pay such damages as may be awarded and to be restrained accordingly.

Provided, that the sum recoverable in respect of any one design shall not exceed rupees fifty thousand.

A person engaging in manufacture and or sale of Fake or spurious auto component will at best be required to pay a damage of Rs. 25000 or Rs. 50,000 as the case may be which is by no means a deterrent.

No criminal punishment is envisaged by the Designs Act and the penalties do not serve as a deterrent.

Th e limitation of all IP laws, copyright act notwithstanding, is that they do not provide for a self starting mechanism where the state machinery monitors, surveys and takes action against traffickers in spurious auto components that can potentially risk safety of general public and their property. Besides, @Criminal law has not been invoked to afford protection against infringement of patent rights.

The same also applies in the case of Design Act. Though society is concerned with protection of patents and designs, criminal law is not employed within the framework of public policy.(@ Intellectual property and Criminal Law by Shri. N.S. Gopalakrishnan, The National Law School of India University, Bangalore).

Another major limitation of the existing IP and other laws is that these provide for no punitive damages for conduct that is "willful and wanton", "with a reckless regard for safety of Consumers". (fake or spurious auto components more often infringe Intellectual property rights). In the famous case of BMW Vs Gore, United States Supreme Court established "guidepost" for assessing the extent of punitive damage. In another leading case State Farm Vs Campbell the United States Supreme Court laid down principle for justifying punitive damages thus: Is the defendant's culpability so reprehensible as to warrant a punitive damage in addition to compensatory damage as a deterrent based on the factors viz.,

1. Whether the harm caused was physical or economical?

2. Whether the conduct evinced an indifference to or a reckless disregard of the health and safety of others?

3. Was the target/victim of the alleged conduct financially vulnerable

4. Whether the conduct was repeated or isolated and

5. Whether the harm was the result of intentional malice, trickery or deceit?" (Reference: Strategies for dealing with the risk of punitive damages by Harvey L. Kaplan and Ms Angela M. Seaton of Shook, Hardy and Bacon LLP).

The third limitation of existing laws is not a shortcoming of the laws by themselves but is owing to the ingenuity of the fakers themselves who manufacture un-banded and unpacked non safe products and escape the clutches of any of the existing I P laws.

EU Directive on General Product Safety

To deal with unscrupulous manufacturers of fake and non conforming products, we need to take a leaf from the EU directive on 'General Product Safety' under which a product that does not meet the definition of a 'safe product' is considered as 'dangerous'. A safe product is any product which, under normal or reasonably foreseeable conditions of use including duration and where applicable, putting into service, installation and maintenance requirements, does not present any risk or only the minimum risks compatible with the product's use, considered to be acceptable and consistent with a high level of protection for the health and safety of persons. Regard shall be had to:

- The characteristics of the product, including its composition, packaging, instructions for assembly and where applicable, for installation and maintenance.
- It's effect on other products, where it is reasonably foreseeable that it will be used with other products.
- The presentation of the Product, the labeling, any warnings and instructions for its use and disposal and any other indication or information regarding the product.
- The categories of consumers at risk when using the product, in particular children and the elderly.

The EU directive imposes a number of obligations on producers and distributors to reduce the risk of 'dangerous products' being placed on the EU market. In particular, Producers must:

- Place only safe products in the market
- Provide consumers with relevant information to enable them to assess risks inherent in the product
- Have systems to enable them to be informed of risks that a product might pose
- Have systems to enable them to take appropriate action to avoid risks (including to trace the marketed products)
- Keep distributors informed of any sample testing or other monitoring activities
- Where appropriate carry out sample testing of marketed products, keep register of complaints and adequately investigate complaints.

- Notify the competent authorities immediately a marketed product is known or should be known to pose unacceptable risks
- Recall of dangerous products by the manufacturers/authorities

Distributors on their part are required to support the directive

- By keeping and making available whatever documents are necessary for tracing the origin of the products (incidentally this is the biggest vacuum in the drive conducted against spurious products in the Indian automotive after market).
- Passing on information on product risks Co-operating with the action taken by the producers and competent authorities
- Notifying the competent authorities immediately a marketed product is known or should be known to pose unacceptable risks
- Under the Directive, national authorities are obliged to take necessary steps to ensure adequate market surveillance of consumer products. (Reference: Product Safety: The New EU Regime by Rod Freeman and John Meltzer of Lowells)

Principles similar to The EU directive on product safety (or conversely in relation to dangerous products) must find an important place in any legislation intended to combat he menace of spurious auto components.

Intellectual Property Rights (Imported Goods) Enforcement Rules, 2007

The Intellectual Property Rights (Imported Goods) Enforcement Rules, 2007, notified on May 07, 2007 seeks to protect IP rights in connection with counterfeit and pirated goods (auto components included) imported into India. IPR Rules, 2007 empowers the Deputy/Assistant Commissioner of Customs as competent authority to seize counterfeit or pirated goods or suspend the clearance of the goods. Customs Department has the additional right to destroy confiscated goods infringing intellectual property rights. Customs Authorities are enabled to take pro active action on their own accord in suspected cases of counterfeiting and piracy. The rules even protect the rights of IP owner against genuine parallel imports as in the case of Samsung Electronics Company Limited and Another vs. G. Choudhary and Another, 2006 (33) PTC 425 (Del). These rules are welcome and its working has to be studied for some years considering that the rules came into force only some three years ago.

Consumers Right of Access to Non-hazardous Product

One of the important features of the United Nation Guidelines for Consumer Protection is that the Consumer should have the right of access to non-hazardous products. Accordingly the General Principles of the said Guidelines mandate governments to protect consumers from hazards to their health and safety, promote and protect economic interests of consumers, facilitate access of consumers to adequate information, promote consumer education, facilitate effective consumer redress and the freedom of consumers to form organizations. The Consumer Protection Act, 1986 addresses some of these General Principles but not adequately when it comes to spurious or fake or counterfeit auto components that can endanger the health, safety and property of the consumers and the general public. The UN guidelines apply to home products as well as to imports.

In the matter of physical safety, the guidelines require the governments to adopt appropriate measures, including legal systems, safety regulations, national and international standards, voluntary standards and maintenance of safety records to ensure that products are safe for their intended or normally foreseeable use. The guidelines further require governments to frame appropriate policies to ensure that if manufacturers or distributors become aware of unforeseen hazards after products are placed on the market, they should notify relevant authorities and as appropriate, the public without delay.

Although the ministry of Consumer affairs, Government of India has expressly adopted the consumers' right to safety, to be informed, to choose, to be heard, to seek redressal and the right to consumer education, the existing laws do not fully address all the issues enshrined in the United Nations Guidelines for Consumer Protection.

In this context it is relevant to note that Product Liability may be objective (strict liability) or based on contract (contractual liability) or tortuous (tort liability) or a crime (criminal liability). Strict liability which is in addition to relief one can seek under the contract law and Law in tort is based on specific product liability law whether general or product wise. Several countries like Belgium, People's Republic of China, Denmark, Germany, Hungary, Ireland have Consumers right of access to non-hazardous product Israel, Japan, Korea, Latvia, Lithuania, Netherlands, Norway, Sweden, Switzerland, The United States of America etc have strict Product Liability law in place (Reference: The International Comparative Legal Guide to Product Liability 2007).

In the absence of a specific law dealing with defective/fake/ spurious products (except in case of specified products like food and drugs) the aggrieved has recourse to the Law of Torts to deal with instances of criminal negligence or to the Indian Penal code in respect of Cheating or such other offenses. But these are no substitute to a product specific law. Besides, the degree of proof is strict in case of criminal proceedings and the onus remains with the complainant.

Barring sector specific or product specific legislation as in the case of food, drugs etc, under the existing laws, there exists no criminal sanctions for manufacture/supply of defective products. *Invariably spurious/counterfeit/fake auto components would qualify as a 'defective or non safe product'. Automotive specific product safety*

Regulations with stringent criminal punishment will go a long way in arresting the manufacture and sale of spurious auto components. This regulation can be conveniently built in the existing Motor Vehicles Act.

The Vehicle Research and Development Establishment, The Automotive Research Association of India, Pune, The Central Machinery Testing and Training Institute, Bundi, The Indian Institute of Petroleum, Dehradun which are government recognized testing agencies under the Central Motor Vehicles Rules.

MOTOR VEHICLES ACT AND RULES

Motor Vehicles Act 1988 was passed to provide inter alias for laying down of standards for the components and parts of motor Vehicles and standards for anti-pollution control devices. Chapter VII of the Act deals with the Construction, Equipment and Maintenance of Motor Vehicles. In terms of Section 110 of the Act, the Central government has the rule making power regulating construction, equipment and maintenance of motor vehicles including, inter alias for,

- brakes and steering gear;
- use of safety glasses including prohibition of the use of tinted safety glasses;
- signaling appliances, lamps and reflectors;
- speed governors;
- emission of smoke, visible vapor, sparks, ashes, grit or oil;
- reduction of noise emitted by or caused by vehicles;
- Safety belts, handle bars or motor cycles, auto-dippers and other equipment's essential for safety of drivers, passengers and other road users.
- Standards of the components used in the vehicle as inbuilt safety devices;

It is often misunderstood that the Act is intended only to regulate completely assembled vehicles and not component used or intended for use in vehicles. It is also believed that the Act does not embrace safety and standards of components made for or sold in the aftermarket. Chapter VII comprises only three sections (109 to 111) but it is one of the most potent sections which can regulate the quality and standards of auto components available in the aftermarket. It is recommended that greater clarity should be provided either by way of notification or by exercise of the rule making power or by suitably amending the section (which is perhaps not necessary). A notification to the effect that Section 109 to 111 of Chapter VII shall equally apply to automotive Components manufactured or sold or serviced in the aftermarket is necessary.

The administration of the Motor Vehicles Act is decentralized at the 'State' level and rightly so. The length and breadth of the country is covered by a Regional Transport Authorities of the respective state.

It is necessary to create a state level enforcement agency with adequate supervisory powers to deal with offences concerning manufacture, storage, packing, distribution and sale of counterfeit or non standard automotive Component. Similar to the weights and measures act, inspectors and other officers should be entrusted with authority and duty to search, seize any non complying auto component and also punish the offenders. Simultaneously the Motor Vehicles Act should lay down standards for more and more safety, pollution and emission related automotive components.

Care should be taken to see that genuine automotive component manufactures are not harassed by the enforcement mechanism.

Alongside it is necessary to install the facility of toll free call number in each district or state which can be contacted by any whistle blower if he or she comes across any one engaged in the business chain of spurious or fake automotive component. A well thought out whistle blower mechanism should be put in place.

THE DRUGS AND COSMETICS ACT

The Drugs and Cosmetics (Amendment) Act, 2008 has amended the provisions of the Drugs and Cosmetics Act, 1940 relating to the offences for manufacture and trade of adulterated and spurious drugs and enhanced the penalties in a significant way by bringing them under the head "serious offences." The amended act also provides for "special courts" for the prosecution of such offences and for grant of compensation to the victims of adulterated and spurious drugs.

In the case of an offence relating to manufacture, sale, distribution, stocking or exhibiting or offering for sale or distribution of "adulterated drug" the period of imprisonment has been enhanced from 1-3 years to 3-5 years and fine has been enhanced from the earlier Rupees 5,000 to Rupees 100,000 or 3 times the value of the drug confiscated, whichever is higher.

In case of offence relating to manufacture, sale, distribution, stocking or exhibiting or offering for sale or distribution of adulterated drug or spurious drug and a drug which when used by any person for his treatment is likely to cause his death or grievous hurt, the period of imprisonment has been enhanced from the present 5 years – imprisonment for life to 10 years – imprisonment for life and fine has been enhanced from the earlier Rupees 10,000 to Rupees 100,000 or 3 times the value of the drug confiscated, whichever is higher.

Another significant change in the Amended Act is that trials for offences relating to trading in sub-standard drugs now start at the level of the Court of Session. The appeals from the Court of Session lie to the High Court and then to the Supreme Court. This change is expected to accelerate the prosecution of these offences.

The amended act also provides for "special courts" for the prosecution of offences relating to adulterated drugs or spurious drugs. The Central Government, or the State Government, in consultation with the Chief Justice of the High Court, are required to designate one or more Courts of Session as "Special Courts" to deal with certain offences such as importation of adulterated drugs, spurious drugs or spurious cosmetics; trading in drugs that fall under the definition of 'spurious drugs'; trading in spurious or adulterated drug which when used by any person for his treatment is likely cause his death or grievous hurt; non-disclosure of the name of the manufacturer by a person who is an agent of the manufacturer; willful obstruction of a Drug Inspector in the exercise of the powers conferred upon him by law; refusal to produce any documents relating to trade of a sub-standard drug in respect of the person who is believed to have committed an offence etc.

Offences that relate to adulterated drugs and spurious drugs are now considered to be cognizable offences. Cognizable offence, under the Code of Criminal Procedure, is an offence for which a police officer does not require a "warrant" (sanction of a Magistrate) to arrest the one who is believed to have committed the offence. These offences are also non-bailable. Previously, most offences fell under the category of non-cognizable and bailable.

The difference between "cognizable" and "non-cognizable" offence is that in case of a cognizable offence, a police officer may arrest an offender without warrant and that in case of a non-cognizable offence a police officer has no authority to arrest an offender without warrant i.e. permission from a magistrate for registration of a criminal case.

Cognizable cases involve criminal offences. Murder, Robbery, Theft, Rioting, Counterfeiting etc. are some examples of cognizable offences.

Non-cognizable offences are criminal infractions, which are considered less serious. Examples of non-cognizable offences include Public Nuisance, Causing Simple Hurt, Assault, Mischief etc.

Under the Code of Criminal Procedure, offences have been classified as 'bailable' and 'non-bailable' offences.

In the case of a bailable offence, if the accused produces proper surety after his arrest, and fulfills other conditions, it is incumbent upon the investigating officer to grant bail and release the accused.

In the case of a non-bailable offence, the Investigating Officer must produce the accused before the Judicial Magistrate/Judge concerned within 24 hours of the arrest. At that time, the accused has a right to apply for bail himself or through his representative/lawyer.

It is recommended that offences relating to manufacture, sale, distribution, packaging, warehousing, transportation and printing of packaging material intended for spurious safety related auto components are made cognizable and non bailable drawing analogy from the Drugs and Cosmetics Act.

Food Adulteration Act

Notwithstanding existing provisions of Sections 272 and 273 of IPC, considering the serious consequences of adulteration of food articles and to effectively combat adulteration of food, the Government of India has enacted "The Prevention of Food Adulteration Act." The act provides for stringent and deterrent actions against those indulging in adulteration/misbranding of food articles by including life imprisonment for adulteration causing grievous hurt and danger to human life.

The act defines "misbranded" article of food, inter-alias, to include an article of food which is an imitation of, or is a substitute for, or resembles in a manner likely to deceive, another article of food under the name of which it is sold or if it is falsely stated to be the product of any place or country or if it is sold by a name which belongs to another article of food or if it is falsely stated to be the product of any place or country or if false claims are made for it upon the label or otherwise or if the package containing it or the label on the package bears the name of a fictitious individual or company as the manufacturer or producer of the article.

Section 7 of the Act inter alias expressly prohibits that no person shall himself or by any person on his behalf, manufacture for sale or store, sell or distribute any adulterated or misbranded food.

Section 14 provides that no manufacturer or distributor of, or dealer in any article of food shall sell article to any vendor unless he also gives a warranty in writing in the prescribed form about the nature and quality of such article to the vendor.

Section 14A of the Act requires every vendor to disclose the name, etc, of the person from whom the article of food was sourced to the food inspector.

Section 16A of the act provides for trial of offences in a summary way.

The act inter alias also provides that in the case of an article of food or adulterant, which when consumed by any person is likely to cause his death or is likely to cause such harm on his body as would amount to grievous hurt within the meaning of section 320 of the Indian Penal code (45 of 1860) imprisonment for a term which shall not be less than three years but which may extend to term of life and with fine.

Under Section 23 of the Act the responsibility of implementation of Prevention of Food Adulteration Act and Rules framed there under vests in the State Governments and Union Territories. Each State Government and Union Territory has created its own structure/organization for implementing of the Act.

Having regard to public health and safety, it is appropriate to treat manufacture, distribution of fake or spurious auto components, particularly those considered as safety related, in the same manner as the manufacture of spurious food products and deserves to be dealt with severely and on similar lines.

It is recommended that provisions concerning prohibition of, manufacture for sale or storage, sale or distribution of spurious auto components, grant of warranty, mandatory disclosure of source of supply, summary trial of offences, enhancement of penalties for offences etc are introduced within the Motor Vehicles Act.

STOP COUNTERFEITING IN MANUFACTURED GOODS ACT

In March 2006 The United States of America passed this law for the following reasons:

- loss of millions of dollars in tax revenue and tens of thousands of jobs because of the manufacture, distribution, and sale of counterfeit goods;
- estimate by the Bureau of Customs and Border Protection that counterfeiting costs the United States $200 billion annually;
- counterfeit automobile parts, including brake pads, cost the auto industry alone billions of dollars in lost sales each year;
- counterfeit products have invaded numerous industries, including those producing auto parts, electrical appliances, medicines, tools, toys, office equipment, clothing, and many other products;
- ties have been established between counterfeiting and terrorist organizations that use the sale of counterfeit goods to raise and launder money;
- ongoing counterfeiting of manufactured goods poses a widespread threat to public health and safety; and
- strong domestic criminal remedies against counterfeiting will support stronger anti-counter feiting provisions in bilateral and international agreements with trading partners.

The reasons set out above are equally relevant in the Indian context.

It is recommended that the Government build into the Motor Vehicles Act provisions similar to "stop Counterfeiting in automotive components" not only to support the automotive Industry but more importantly in consumer and public interest.

Bureau of Indian Standards Act (BIS)

The Product Certification Scheme of BIS aims at providing Third Party Guarantee of quality, safety and reliability of products to the ultimate customer. The certification allows the licensees to use the popular ISI Mark. Presence of ISI certification mark known as Standard Mark on a product is an assurance of conformity to the specifications. The conformity is ensured by regular surveillance of the licensee's performance by surprise inspections and testing of samples, drawn both from the market and factory.

The BIS product certification scheme is essentially voluntary in nature which provides general rules for third party certification system of determining conformity with product standards through initial testing and assessment of a factory quality management system and its acceptance followed by surveillance that takes into account the factory Quality management system and the testing of samples from the factory and the open market.

Although, the scheme itself is voluntary in nature, the Government of India, on considerations of public health and safety, security, infrastructure requirements and mass consumption has enforced mandatory certification on various products through Orders issued from time to time under various Acts. While BIS continues to grant licenses on application, the enforcement of compulsory certification is done by the notified authorities.

Automotive Components is one of the several operational areas identified by BIS for product certification. Till date automotive tyres have been subjected to mandatory BIS certification as per details given:

The enforcing authority for the above mandatory certification is yet to be specified.

Chapter VII of the Central Motor Vehicles Rules 1999, concerning the construction, equipment and maintenance of Motor Vehicles prescribes Indian Standards for brakes (Rule 96), steering gears (Rule 98), safety glass (rule 100), windscreen wiper (Rule 101), Speedometer (Rule 117), Speed governor (Rule 118), Horns (Rule 119) etc. *It is recommended these standards should also apply to the said parts sold in the aftermarket. Likewise Rule 124 or the rules concerning safety standards of components should be made applicable to components sold in the aftermarket.*

It is also recommended that many more safety related automotive component should be brought under the purview of mandatory BIS Certification. ACMA can play a major role in identifying such auto components.

The enforcing authorities could be the respective state governments through their existing machinery established under the Motor Vehicles Act who in turn can take the support of Automotive Research Association of India and other certifying agencies under the Motor Vehicles Act.

Compliance Marketing

It is recommended that a compliance marking of auto components may be considered once the pre requisites for the same are in place. By affixing such mark on a product, the manufacturer declares to the public at large the conformity of the product with all of the legal requirements as to product Quality and standards including health, safety and environment.

Consumer Education

There is a need for continuous on going exercise to educate the consumers and general public on the harmful effects of fake auto components, to distinguish fake from genuine and promote the use of genuine auto components. The Consumer Protection Unit (upbhogta Jagran) of the Ministry of consumer affairs should take specific initiatives in co-operation with ACMA and other automotive organizations to educate customers in this respect through country vide media program under their Jago Grahak Campaign.

Name of the Standard	IS number	Product
Pneumatic Tyres and Tubes for Automotive Vehicles (Quality Control) Order, 2009 Vide Ministry of Commerce and Industry (DIPP) Notification S.O. No. 2953(E) dated 19th November 2009 (Date of Implementation: 19 May 2010)	IS 7815627	Automotive Vehicles- Pneumatic Tyres for two and three-wheeled motor vehicles- Specification
	IS 7915633	Automotive Vehicles- Pneumatic Tyres for passenger car vehicles– Diagonal and radial ply- Specification
	IS 8015636	Automotive Vehicles- Pneumatic Tyres for commercial vehicles- Diagonal and radial ply- Specification
	IS 8113098	Automotive Vehicles-Tubes for Pneumatic Tyres-Specification.

It is recommended that the Ministry of Consumer Affairs educates the general public who are either active or passive users of automotive vehicles and consequently also of the components. Consumer education can go a long way in neutralizing the efforts of those engaged in manufacture and distribution of fakes or spurious auto components.

Prescription

1. Re-orient Motor Vehicles Act also as Automotive Components anti counterfeit and Product Safety Law. Rephrase the preamble to the act appropriately.

2. Define counterfeit or spurious auto components in a comprehensive way within the Motor Vehicles Act.

3. The Motor Vehicles Act also comprehensively define what constitutes manufacturing, packing, trading, distributing, warehousing, repacking, transportation, printing of packing material etc for/of fake/defective/spurious automotive components.

4. Provide in the Motor Vehicles Act that offences in connection with manufacture, packing, sale, stocking, distribution etc., of spurious auto components will be considered cognizable and non-bailable and also for summary trial of such offences.

5. Prescribe stringent punishment in terms of higher financial penalty and imprisonment for those engaged in spurious auto component activity.

6. Accord to the state a pro active role and a 'suo motto' authority to monitor, initiate prosecution for offences in connection with the manufacture, packaging, sale, stocking, distribution etc., of spurious auto components and for this purpose establish machinery within the Motor Vehicles Act.

7. Mandate that supply of safe auto components as enshrined in the Motor Vehicles Act and Rules apply not only the manufacturer but to all intermediaries engaged in the automotive business chain from manufacture to supply to the ultimate customer.

8. Enlarge the role of government recognized testing agencies under the Central Motor Vehicles Rules to also support action for arresting business in spurious auto components.

9. Bring clarity that Motor Vehicles Act is intended not only to regulate completely assembled vehicles and parts fitted to completely assembled vehicles but also to components used or intended for use in vehicles supplied by or procured from the automotive aftermarket. Notify that Section 109 to Section 111 of Chapter VII shall equally apply to automotive components manufactured or sold or serviced in the aftermarket.

10. Establish within the Motor Vehicles Act, State level enforcement agency with adequate supervisory powers to deal with persons engaging in the manufacture, storage, packing, distribution and sale of counterfeit or non standard automotive Component.

11. Introduce a system of Compliance marking by self declaration.

12. Establish state level whistle blower mechanism of toll free call number which can be contacted by anyone who wishes to blow the whistle.

13. Prohibit grant of warranty for spurious goods.

14. Mandate trade to compulsory discloser of source of procurement/supply of spurious auto components.

15. BIS to identify many more safety related automotive components for compulsory BIS Certification, in consultation with ACMA.

16. Ministry of Consumer Affairs to educate the consumers and general public on the danger to life and property due to use of spurious auto components and the need to use original automotive parts.

Note: The prescriptions do not affect the right of the aggrieved to take action under any existing legislation.

Chapter 10
Conclusion

WHITE PAPER ON BLACK MONEY HAS MANY HOLES

The White Paper on black money, it seems, is a total whitewash. From bikini to black hole, it has been criticized left, right and centre. Some even call it a thick black paper blocking the names of black money holders.

Presented by Finance Minister Pranab Mukherjee in the Lok Sabha this week, the White Paper does not provide official estimate of black money nor does it disclose the names of tax offenders with large funds stashed overseas.

It debunks the commonly-held notion that hundreds of billions of dollars of Indian money is stashed illegally in Swiss banks, saying most of this money may have come back home as FDI flows routed through low-tax countries such as Mauritius and Singapore, and via hawala and stock market transactions involving participatory notes and global depository receipts.

It also describes as "baseless allegations" the widely-circulated figures about black money—one offered by US-based Global Financial Integrity (213.2 billion dollar outflow between 1948 and 2008) and the other by International Monetary Fund (88 billion dollars during 1971-97).

The right-wing Bharatiya Janata Party (BJP) has called it a "non-paper," with its leader Jaswant Singh likening it to a bikini that conceals all the essentials and reveals only the non-essentials.

He says it is an opportunity wasted to cleanse politics as the documents fails to reveal the quantum of black money made by corrupt politicians and the use of such funds in politics.

Many feel that political parties are the biggest guzzler of cash, and reforming poll funding will be the key to curbing black money. The Left parties find the White Paper a futile exercise without any clear-cut directions for action to unearth the black money. Some call the white paper a black hole. Both Right and Left have taken on the Government for stating that the bank deposits of Indians in Swiss accounts decreased from Rs. 23,373 crore in 2006 to Rs. 9,295 crore in 2010, and want to know where that money has gone.

Lawyer Prashant Bhushan, a member of Team Anna, says the Government is not serious about fighting corruption as the White Paper does not mention the steps to be taken to stop non-transparent financial instruments such as participatory notes, and its intention to change the treaty with Mauritius which legalises black money.

The Government's suggestions for a no-objection certificate from the tax department on immoveable property transactions and the limit on the cash an individual can hold have also come in for sharp criticism on the ground that these will bring back the days of the inspector raj.

The White Paper, however, rightly pin points real estate as the biggest generator of black money, and suggests deducting tax at source on all real estate deals and making it a precondition to registering a property. It also wants a cap on the number of companies that operate out of the same premises and the number of companies in which a person can become a director. It also rightly mentions that most of unaccounted money is invested in Gold and jewellery, and suggests amending the customs and income tax Act to check such transactions.

It also makes out a case for encouraging payment through debit and credit cards to keep a proper audit trail for transactions. Apart from making it compulsory for the private sector to pay salaries through the banking channels—cheques—, the Government can also deliberate providing tax incentives for use of credit/debit cards as practiced in Republic of Korea, the Paper says.

On black money stashed in foreign bank accounts, the Government may consider a voluntary disclosure of income scheme, a one time amnesty scheme, on the lines of the mechanism adopted by developed countries such as the US, the UK, France and Germany, it says. But rather than more stringent tax laws and policing networks, what is needed is a more simplified tax structure that reduces cost of compliance and suppresses the urge of avoiding taxes.

Yashwardhan Joshi

Counterfeit and Smuggling

RESEARCH REPORT FINDINGS

A study done by "Thought Arbitrage" sponsored by FICCI (Federation of Indian Chamber of Commerce and Industries) committee against smuggling and counterfeiting Activities destroying the economy (CASCADE) to get some authentic agenda on the subject came up with the following findings.

Auto Components: A grey market of 29.6% resulting in sales loss of Rs 9,198 crores to the industry.

Alcohol: A grey market of 10.2% resulting in a sales loss of Rs 5,626 crores to the legitimate industry.

Computer hardware: A grey market of 26.4% resulting in sales loss of Rs 4,725 crores to the computer hardware industry.

FMCG (Personal care): A grey market of 25.9% resulting in sales loss of Rs 15,035 crores to the legitimate industry.

Packaged foods: A grey market of 23.4% resulting in a sales loss of Rs 20,377 crores to the industry.

Mobile phones: A grey market of 20.8% resulting in sales loss of Rs 9,042 crores to the industry.

Tobacco: A grey market of 15.7% resulting in a sales loss of Rs 8,965 crores to the legitimate industry.

Other sectors: The Ministry of Health and Family Welfare, Government if India, estimates that 5% of drugs in the country are counterfeit, while another 0.3% is spurious. Taking 5% as the grey market, the sales loss to industry stands at Rs.4,274 crores.

CRIMINAL CONSEQUENCES

Counterfeiting has attracted the attention of criminal networks, as the activities are highly profitable and carry relatively low-risks.

IACC, on tracking the increasing influx of terrorist organizations into the lucrative underworld of criminal counterfeiting and piracy, is convinced that genuine and credible links exist because of anonymity, high profitability and non-traceability of such activities. Counterfeiters may use these activities as a means of potential attack by using deadly chemicals, poisons or biological toxins in pharmaceutical sector. The bombing of the World Trade Centre in 1993 is now though to have been partly funded by the sale of counterfeit textiles from an outlet on Broadway.

The growth in the role of criminal networks in counterfeiting and piracy is a concern for economies as it can undermine civil society by providing those networks with the resources required to finance a range of illicit activities, in a corrupt and organized manner. Society's security is increasingly getting affected on account of nexus between criminals and counterfeiters as "super-normal" profits and slush funds generated from such criminal counterfeiting operations quickly find their way to the underworld and go on to fund crime syndicates. Low risk of prosecution and enormous profit potential continue to make criminal counterfeiting and piracy attractive for such enterprises to finance other, more violent crimes.

Conclusions

The estimated sales loss to the industry in the seven selected sectors amounts to Rs. 72,969 crores and the consequential loss to the exchequer Rs. 26,190 crores.

A limited study was conducted on pharmaceutical and other FMCG sectors. Initial estimates of sales loss to industry in these sectors is around Rs. 29,307 crores. Hence, the overall estimate of sales loss to industry, exceeds Rs. 1,00,000 crores annually.

Annexure I

The World's Local ~~Bank~~ Money Launderette

The US Senate report charging HSBC with active money-laundering has created worldwide concern. But here's the thing, there's a major banking scandal every 18 months or so. All the concern amounts to little

:: Bennett Voyles

A few years ago, HSBC ran an award-winning series of ads at airports that took the same photos labelled with different points of view. A glass half-full or half-empty. A high-heeled shoe and a hot pepper titled pain/pleasure and pleasure/pain.

That campaign is now long gone but if the allegations of a recent US Senate report are true, they might also have run photos of drug dealers and terrorists captioned criminals/customers.

During the decade after 9/11 and the passage of the USA Patriot Act, the report suggests that HSBC really has been trying to be the World's Local Bank, as it branded itself until recently. A scathing 335-page report released on July 17 by the US Senate's Permanent Subcommittee on Investigations concluded that the London-headquartered bank had helped finance illegal drug traffic in Mexico, terrorism in West Asia and money laundering almost everywhere.

Perhaps even more surprisingly, the report is called a case study – implying that HSBC isn't a special case. One expert agrees the situation described is not unique. "You could almost substitute the name of any other international bank into this HSBC thing," says Jason Sharman, a professor at Griffith University in Brisbane, Australia, and an expert on money laundering and political corruption.

Among the more incendiary allegations against the sprawling bank, whose 300,000 employees manage $2.5 trillion in assets for 89 million customers in over 80 countries:

■ Served as the banker for over 2,000 bearer share corporation – a corporate form in which the identity of the shareholder is unknown and verified only by physical ownership of the shares. A kind of corporate finance equivalent of the proverbial numbered Swiss bank account, bearer shares are a structure Sharman describes as "the money launderer's best friend."
■ Failed to correct serious deficiencies in its Mexican anti-money laundering efforts between 2002 and 2010, including a policy that treated Mexico as a low-risk country for money laundering, despite an ongoing drug war that has killed over 46,000 people in the past five years.
■ Cleared $290 million in travellers cheques over a four-year period deposited by Russians into 30 accounts of a regional Japanese bank, supposedly in connection with a used car business.
■ Conducted over $19 billion in transactions involving persons in Iran, Cuba, Myanmar, North Korea and Sudan all countries on the US list countries with which banks are prohibited to do business.
■ Concealed 85% of nearly 25,000 transactions with

The Economic Times (Magazine)
August 05-11, 2012

Iran between 2002 and 2007, in violation of US law.

David Bagley, head of group compliance since 2002, stepped down at the July 17 Senate hearing at which the report was released, noting drily that, "Despite the best efforts and intentions of many dedicated professionals, HSBC has fallen short of our own expectations and the expectations of our regulators."

Too Big to Succeed
A number of factors seem to have led HSBC to the bright lights of a Senate committee hearing last week.
Simply keeping track of HSBC's vast and complicated operation seems to have been a challenge. "Some of these banks have grown to be too large and complex for anyone — CEO or executive management team — to really get their hands around," says James Lam, a Wellesley, Massachusetts-based risk management expert, who coined the term chief risk officer and served as CRO for both GE Capital and Fidelity Investments in the 1990s.
However, complexity was far from being the only problem at HSBC. Lam says the essential challenges of managing bank risk are the same whether you're a community bank or a global bank. Size and geographic dispersion adds to the challenge, but the factors aren't insurmountable. "There's not some cliff you fall off and it's impossible to manage," he says.
The compliance function seems to have been deeply troubled at HSBC. Despite an elaborate, alphabet-soup of committees reporting and updating risks — the group website, for example, mentions a Global Operational Risk and Control Committee ("GORCC"), a Group Audit Committee ("GAC") and a Group Risk Committee ("GRC"), all of whom have some risk-management functions — in practice, local bankers seem to have called the shots.
The report notes a lot of danger signs within HSBC's compliance office: lack of resources, a huge backlog of complaints, a vast number of suspect transactions, and high turnover in the compliance office. "All these things are real red flags," Lam says.
Lack of resources seems to have been a key problem in the US compliance operation. The report includes a quote from an email of Wyndham Clark AML officer in 2010, who wrote after only a few months on the job — and a few months before he quit: "We are in dire straights (sic) right now over backlogs, and decisions are being made by those who don't understand the risks or consequences of their decisions!!!"
Although ostensibly driven by a drive to cut the budget, the short-handedness also seems to have reflected a deeper level of management contempt for the compliance function. "The fact that their perspectives were seen as advice as opposed to approval really speaks volumes in terms of the standing of compliance within that institution," Lam says. "...In an institution where risk and compliance is respected as an overall function, compliance officers usually get the final say in terms of who do we do business with, what kinds of actions are permitted."

In the end, HSBC's non-compliance with regulations came down to a management choice: "Making money and pleasing the customer overrode compliance issues and knowing the customer," Lam says.

Sorting for Character
An over-emphasis on technical knowledge in hiring risk and compliance officers is often part of the problem in companies that have difficulties with compliance, according to Lam. Sometimes, companies hiring risk and compliance officers "tend to focus too much on the technical skills as opposed to the integrity, character, and courage of the individual," Lam says.

HSBC: A snapshot

300,000 employees
Manages $2.5 trillion for 89 mn customers across 80 countries

> HSBC's compliance office had lot of danger signs within: lack of resources, huge backlog of complaints, a vast number of suspect transactions, & high turnover

One question at the interview is all it would take to make sure that the prospective compliance officer had the courage to really push back, Lam says: "Tell me some conflicts that you've had in the past and how did you resolve those conflicts. If they can't come up with anything, that's a real warning indicator," he says with a grin.

Making money and pleasing the customer overrode compliance issues and knowing the customer

James Lam
Risk Management Expert

Irregular Regulation
Regulators who didn't regulate may have also contributed to HSBC's weak anti-money laundering regime.
"You really can't rely on that framework to catch some of these issues. We saw that with the Libor scandal, we've seen that in this case, we saw that with JP Morgan Chase's CIO office," Lam says, naming two of the highest profile bank disasters of the past six months.
This may be particularly true for a heavyweight such as HSBC. One ironic consequence of the success of the anti-money laundering campaigns of the past decade is that it may have actually increased the intensity of laundering in the world's financial capitals, according to Sharman.
The reason is political. While the Cayman Islands may have no pull in London and Washington, the City and Wall Street do have the political heft to push back against regulators, Sharman says. As a result, regulators have been more successful in cleaning up the tax havens and dodgy banks on the periphery but left the more politically protected centre more or less alone. "Regulation, like politics, is the art of the possible," he explains.
For example, Sharman cites the bearer shares mentioned frequently in the report, which are almost universally considered a bad thing by anti-money laundering groups, Sharman says. "You really have to stretch" to find a legitimate reason to use them, he says.
Although the Senate report rails against bearer shares, they're not actually hard to find, even now: despite their bad name, Sharman says "the money launderer's best friend" can still be purchased legally in England and Wales for £140.

Same Song, Second Verse
What happens now? Beyond a variety of measures specifically suggested for HSBC, the Senate report writers recommended stepping up regulatory enforcement against banks that seem to be violating anti-money laundering rules, treating such problems not as a consumer matter but as a more serious question of the bank's safety and soundness.
However, Sharman is sceptical much of anything will happen. "We've had a lot of these damning reports before and the level of change has been much less than you might think," he says.
Outside of a number of suits against HSBC, Sharman is sceptical that the Senate's indictment will change much in the banking world. In his view, bank domination of the regulatory agencies tends to make any real change unlikely.
Roughly every 18 months or so, he says, some new banking scandal usually arises among one of the major international banks. Afterwards, the banks all keep conducting business as usual. "We've been here before," Sharman says. ■

The author, a Paris-based business writer, is a columnist for ET Magazine

The Economic Times (Magazine)
August 05-11, 2012

Annexure II

The Simple Guide to Money Laundering

Money laundering, as both law enforcers and launderers will tell you, is complex. *ET Magazine* sifts through masses of information to list the whos, whys, whats and hows of the crime

:: Shantanu Nandan Sharma

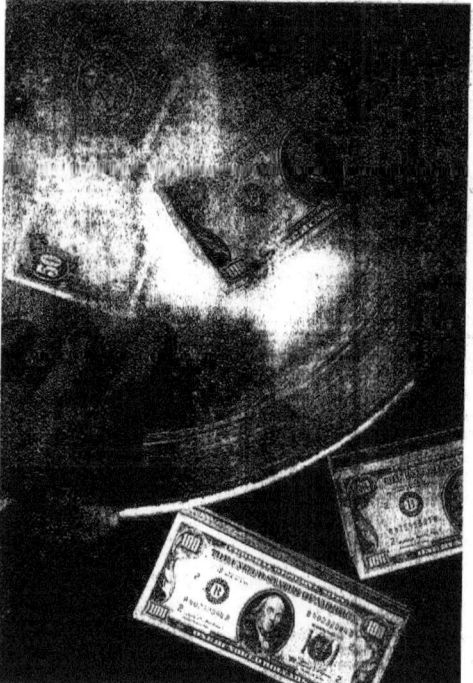

Who is a Money Launderer?

The bookish definition would go something like this: whosoever attempts to indulge or knowingly assists or is actually involved in any activity connected with "proceeds of crime" and projecting it as untainted property is a money launderer. Simply put, money laundering is the process of concealing the source of illegally earned money. Anybody who does this is a money launderer.

The Birth of the Word "Money Laundering"

American gangsters in the country's prohibition era were looking for ways to stash the massive profits they earned from bootlegging. Hoarding cash had its risks, so the gangsters looked to start businesses. One of them was gambling, which led to the growth of Las Vegas, among other hubs. The other business which found favour with the gangsters was laundries. The profits of these two ventures were used to conceal the origin of where the money was really coming from.

Two Myths

✗ **Myth:** Converting black money into white is money laundering.
✓ **Reality:** If the launderer simply conceals income and violates I-T Act, he will not necessarily be booked for money laundering. He or she can be booked only if one of the 30 acts (statutes) which are included in the Prevention of Money Laundering Act is violated.

✗ **Myth:** Money launderers indulge in big-ticket scams.
✓ **Reality:** If someone makes a gain of ₹30 lakh or above by violating any of the 24 acts, like Air (Prevention and Control of Pollution) Act, SEBI Act, Prevention of Corruption Act, it will be considered a case of money laundering.

$2 trillion

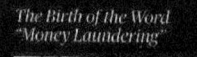

The sum laundered globally, according to the United Nations Office on Drugs and Crime (UNODC). This is about 3% of the world GDP.

The Economic Times (Magazine)
August 05-11, 2012

ANNEXURES

How Money Launderers are Spotted?

Banks, financial institutions and intermediaries are obligated, by law, to keep an eye on such transactions. In India, for example, if a suspected case of money laundering is spotted, the financial institution needs to inform the Financial Intelligence Unit-India (FIU-IND), an enforcement agency.

The FAQs

Why Should Banks Co-operate and Disclose Client Data?

According to Prevention of Money Laundering Act (PMLA), the director of FIU-IND can impose fines on banks and other financial institutions if they fail to detect or conceal wrongdoings.

Who Investigates Money-laundering Cases? And How?

The Enforcement Directorate carries out investigations. The ED is also empowered to attach property of entities involved in money laundering. The investigation begins with filing an Enforcement Case Information Report (ECIR), which is comparable with an FIR. The Adjudicating Authority under PMLA then decides whether the attachment is valid or not. The courts take the final call on punishment and confiscation of property from the money launderers.

What's the Punishment?

Rigorous imprisonment of no less than 3 years and up to 7 years. The PMLA Amendment Bill which is currently in Parliament has proposed that the jail term should go up to 10 years.

Prominent Money Laundering Cases

₹223 Cr
Kalaignar TV (DMK first family)

₹202 Cr
Satyam Computers' founder B Ramalinga Raju

₹168 Cr
Former minister of Jharkhand Anosh Ekka

₹112 Cr
Former CM of Jharkhand Madhu Koda

1,437 Total number of money laundering cases in India registered for investigation

131 Total number of cases where attachment of properties is confirmed

₹1,214 Cr Worth of properties attached so far in money laundering cases in India

₹30 lakh Minimum threshold limit of tainted money for a money laundering case to be filed. Exceptions are serious crimes like terrorism & narcotics

22 The number of persons arrested in India in money laundering cases so far

30 The number of Acts, the violation of which attracts money laundering cases

---

How it Works?

Indian investigators tracking scams such as 2G, Commonwealth Games and Madhu Koda suspect the following as the favourite route for shifting ill-gotten money

Tainted money

Over the years, money will be ploughed back through investments in India

Shell companies floated in Dubai, Singapore and Mauritius

Investments in British Virgin Island, Cayman Islands etc.

Thanks to the banking system, the travel time of millions of dollars across a few continents is just a few hours. But to recover the same, India has to go through legal processes including inking of treaties with each country.

India Joins Battle Against Money Laundering

India joined as 34th member of Financial Action Task Force (FATF) in June 2010. This is expected to help India trace terror funds and prosecute money laundering offences

India joined the Asia Pacific Group (APG) against money laundering. Each hosted its annual meet in 2011

India gained membership of Eurasian Group (EAG) in December 2010. The group is a network of Financial Intelligence Units (FIUs) across the world

New Delhi joined Egmont Group in 2007.

How They Did It

Mohammad Fahad Hai

A Pakistani national belonging to Al-Badr terrorist outfit

Amount Attached
₹50,492 out of the total bank transaction of ₹12 lakh

Modus Operandi
Hai arrived in Mumbai by flight No. PIA 275 from Karachi on February 25, 2006 and left for Calicut by bus on the same night. He moved to Mysore in May 2006 where he stayed with his half-brother. He then opened a savings account in a private Indian bank by submitting a driving licence procured using fake documents. Funds worth ₹1208,116 were transferred from UAE and Qatar. Money also came in through hawala channels during July-October, 2006.

End Game
Hai was arrested by Vijayanagar Police on October 26, 2006. Sections of IPC and Arms Act were slapped. ED provisionally attached ₹50,492 which remained in his account at the time of arrest. The criminal case against him is continuing. Hai is now in jail.

City Limouzines (India) Pvt Ltd

A company set up in 2002 to do business in leasing of vehicles

Amount Attached
₹5.6 crore

Modus Operandi
The company with its subsidiaries floated a scheme called "own a car and earn money from home". Investors forked out a specific sum, using which the company was supposed buy a vehicle. Investors were wooed with a high rate of return of 48% per year. During the scheme period, the investors were promised a monthly fee. Eventually, most of it existed only on paper. Over 25,000 customers were signed on but only 2,200 vehicles were purchased. Thirteen firms from Surat gave bulk orders worth ₹65 crore.

End Game
One of the duped customers filed a complaint in Mumbai in August 2007. Chargesheet were filed against the chairman and other directors of the firm. Sections of IPC were imposed. The IPC is an Act under PMLA, the violation of which constitutes money laundering.

The Economic Times (Magazine)
August 05-11, 2012

Annexure III

WILL WE ACHIEVE FREEDOM FROM BLACK MONEY?

What is black money? It arises from incomes not disclosed to the govt to avoid taxes or because of the corrupt ways by which the wealth was acquired

How big is the problem? Think tanks are finalising a report on estimates of black money. Global Financial Integrity estimated that Indians had stashed $462 billion (₹25.4 lakh crore) in overseas tax havens between 1948-2008

If this money was taxed at 30%, it would generate ₹7.6 lakh crore. Five possible ways to put this to use:

Give it to 405 million poor households | Build 170,000-km of national expressways | Super speciality hospital in each dist | Offer medical insurance to senior citizens | Jobs for all poor rural households

PANEL SUGGESTS SERIES OF MEASURES TO COMBAT GRAFT

HT Correspondent
letters@hindustantimes.com

NEW DELHI: From an early setting of the lokpal and lokayuktas to crack down on benami transactions, encouragement of credit cards to a compliance scheme for bringing back slush funds stashed abroad, a government panel has proposed a wide range of measures to combat black money in report that was released in the backdrop of a series of anti-corruption protests.

"Institutions of lokpal and lokayukta may be put in place at the earliest, in the Centre and states, to expedite investigations into cases of corruption and bring the guilty to justice," the committee said.

The committee, set up in May last year to suggest measures to curb black money, has recommended strengthening of laws that include increasing the maximum jail term from seven to 10 years for government officials found guilty of corruption.

"One of the ways to get assets/money held abroad into the national mainstream is through a compliance scheme," said the report of a committee headed by the central board of direct taxes (CBDT) chairman.

The recommendation will likely rekindle the debate whether the government was planning to offer a fresh immunity scheme to tax offenders.

The last such offer — Voluntary Disclosure of Income Scheme (VDIS) — was introduced in the 1997-98 budget.

The report has recommended the immediate setting up of a national tax tribunal mandated with sweeping judicial powers to clamp down on illegal transactions. The proposal has been pending since two decades due to differences between finance and law ministries.

Hindustan Times
Wednesday, 15 August 2012

Annexure IV

₹565cr black money stashed in France

New Delhi: Undisclosed income of Indians totalling Rs 565 crore has been detected in France, according to income tax authorities, indicating that the Double Taxation Avoidance Agreement is showing results.

The figure was disclosed as part of the exchange of information clause of the DTAA that India shares with France.

In 219 cases, the tax authorities detected undisclosed income totalling Rs 565 crore and taxes amounting to Rs 181 crore have already been realized, the CBDT told Parliament's Public Accounts Committee (PAC) recently.

In a presentation on NRI taxation, the central board of direct taxes (CBDT) said that 30,765 pieces of domestic information about suspicious transactions have been obtained by field intelligence units which are under investigation by respective agencies.

The PAC was informed that this year, New Delhi has commenced tax information exchange agreements (TIEA) with 25 new jurisdictions.

As a result of these exchange agreements, requests from field officers to foreign tax authorities have increased from 39 in 2008-09 to 386 in 2011-13. Till June 30, 120 such requests have been made, the presentation said.

The CBDT said that at the beginning of 2009, India had 78 DTAAs, 75 of which do not have provision for exchange of banking information. With six new agreements coming into force, India now has a total of 84 such agreements with foreign countries. PTI

The figure was disclosed as part of the Double Taxation Avoidance Agreement that India shares with France

The Times of India
Monday, 30 July 2012

Annexure V

Black Money Figures Much Inflated: Govt

A Black Hole?

WHITE PAPER...

1. **Does not** offer official estimate of black money
2. **Does not** disclose names of those with assets overseas
3. **Silent on** black money role in poll funding

PROBLEM AREAS
- Real estate, jewellery, financial sector, public procurement, trade, tax havens key black money sources
- ₹9,295 cr held by Indians in Swiss a/cs in 2010, down from ₹23,273 cr in 2006
- Vodafone tax case clear misuse of corporate structure to avoid taxes
- FDI, PNs, GDRs may have been used to bring back funds

WAY AHEAD
- POSSIBILITY of a one-time amnesty scheme to increase disclosure and recover tax
- GOLD DEPOSIT scheme to encourage disclosure of black money stocked as gold

OUR BUREAU
NEW DELHI

The government has suggested in its first-ever official document on black money that a lot of the illicit cash stashed away overseas over the years may have come back into the country as investments, seeking to debunk the commonly-held notion that hundreds of billions of dollars of Indian money was held illegally in Swiss banks.

The document listed participatory notes (PNs), foreign direct investment (FDI) flows routed through low-tax countries and complex corporate structures as possible contributors to the scourge, but steered clear of naming offenders or putting an estimate on black money, provoking critics to slam it as more of a whitewash than a white paper.

The White Paper on Black Money significantly singled out the Vodafone tax case as an example of misuse of corporate structure to avoid paying taxes, further proof of the intensity of the finance ministry's feelings on its tax dispute with the UK firm and suggesting a compromise was unlikely.

Presented by Finance Minister Pranab Mukherjee in Parliament, the document said illicit money parked outside India may have been brought back as FDI through Mauritius and Singapore and via stock market transactions involving participatory notes and global depository receipts, indicating a tighter scrutiny of these inflows in the future.

The release of the white paper, a day before the third anniversary of the UPA government, comes when the ruling coalition has been mostly on the defensive in its second term in office, buffeted by a series of scandals, popular anti-corruption agitations and scathing court judgments.

Not helping the government is the commonly-held notion that hundreds of billions of dollars have been spirited out of the country and stashed away overseas. US-based Global Financial Integrity, a non-profit research body that has long crusaded against illegal capital flight, said in 2010 that India had been drained of $462 billion between 1948 and 2008.

But the white paper said some of these numbers were over the top and baseless.

"Some of the widely-circulated figures about black money of Indians stashed abroad are baseless exaggerations," it said.

FOLLOW THE MONEY ►► SEE EDIT

RELATED REPORTS ►► 13

Scathing Criticism of Report ►► 10

Cong Must Take the Lead & Reform Political Funding

ET VIEW

The white paper on black money has many suggestions about how to stem the flow of illicit wealth, but forgets to mention the biggest guzzler of cash in the system: political parties. A shift to a GST will help, as will a reasonable and transparent regime of direct taxation. Plugging loopholes like participatory notes can't do any harm. But reforming campaign finance will be the one key measure to judge the administration's seriousness about cracking down on black money. The Congress is India's oldest and biggest party. It should lead by example and make the first move to clean up political funding.

The Economic Times
Thrusday, 22 May 2012

Scathing Criticism of Report

▶▶ From Page 1

There is strong likelihood that substantial amount of such money transferred abroad illicitly might have returned to India through illicit means," the white paper said.

It cited the case of a widely circulated 2006 report attributed to an entity called the Swiss Banking Association, which said Indians had $1,456 billion stashed away overseas. The white paper said actual checks showed no such organisation existed and the money held by Indians in Swiss banks was less than Rs 10,000 crore ($2 billion).

All this did little to silence the government's critics, who were especially scathing about its failure to give out an estimate of black money and disclose the names of tax offenders with large fund stashed overseas.

"This white paper is in reality a non-paper. It is rather like a bikini as it conceals all the essentials and reveals only the non-essentials," said senior BJP leader Jaswant Singh. "The shortcomings include no reliable quantification of illegal money." The government has tasked three domestic research institutions with arriving at estimates of black money. Their reports are expected later this year.

"I would have been happy if I could have included the conclusions of reports of three premier institutions that have been tasked to quantify the magnitude of black money," Mukherjee wrote in the foreword to the 108-page white paper.

The government had agreed to bring out the white paper during the debate over black money and corruption forced by Anna Hazare's anti-graft campaign.

The government said it was bound by tax treaties not to disclose the names of tax offenders with funds overseas.

But this failed to cut ice with another of its bitter critics, yoga guru Baba Ramdev, who called the explanation hogwash. "Lack of political will and the government's lopsided intention is clearly getting reflected in its policies when it says it has no jurisdiction on foreign laws," he said.

Anna Hazare's associate, activist lawyer Prashant Bhushan, said the white paper showed the government had not handled the issue seriously. "If the government was serious about curbing illicit money, they should have taken steps to absolutely stop non-transparent financial instruments like participatory notes. Also, the treaty with Mauritius that legalises black money should have been changed," he said. Official data shows Mauritius accounted for 41.8% of total FDI inflows of $54,227 million into India between April 2000 and March 2011.

During the same period, Singapore accounted for $11,895 million, or 9.17%, of the total inflows.

"Mauritius and Singapore with their small economies cannot be the sources of such huge investments," the white paper noted. "The ultimate beneficiaries/investors through the PN route can be Indians and the source of their investment may be black money generated by them," it added, raising credibility over two of the biggest sources of capital flows into India.

Experts said the problem was likely to be in foreign direct investment through the automatic route, but cautioned that future regulations to plug loopholes should be done in a manner so as not to hurt investor sentiment at a time markets are wobbly and the currency is under pressure. The government's budget proposals for 2012-13, especially the General Anti-Avoidance Rules (GAAR), spooked the markets, forcing it to delay their implementation by a year.

"The problem largely lies in instances of FDI through the automatic route and the current reporting mechanisms may be modified to address this. But it should not create hurdles for genuine investors," said Akash Gupt, executive director at PricewaterhouseCoopers.

The white paper was mostly silent on the links between black money and political funding, which some experts have long cited as the source of corruption and generation of illicit funds. It said the government could consider a one-time amnesty or a gold scheme as viable means to catalyse voluntary disclosure and tax recovery. Citing successful implementation of such schemes by countries such as the US, UK, France and Germany, the paper said the government could explore partial benefit schemes that provide immunity from prosecution in lieu of voluntary disclosure along with payment of taxes, interest and penalty.

"In view of the increasing capacity of tax administration to access information from foreign jurisdiction... a similar scheme (amnesty) targeted at black money stashed abroad can be a one-time option," the paper noted.

It also made a case for tracking bullion and jewellery transactions, encouraging payment through debit and credit cards and prevent misuse of "off market" and "dabba trading" on equities and commodities market. It also said real estate reforms would be essential to curb the use of black money in the sector.

Non-profit organisations also came in for special mention in the document, suggesting that they could see reduced tax privileges and stricter regulatory regime in the future.

Annexure VI

Buying property, jewellery? Govt may ask for receipts

NO GREYS Voluntary disclosure of big buys among proposals to curb black money

ht SPECIAL

Gaurav Choudhury and Nagendra Sharma
■ letters@hindustantimes.com

NEW DELHI: The government may make mandatory the disclosure of high-value purchases such as property and jewellery. Stung by growing public outrage over corruption, finance minister Pranab Mukherjee will on Monday spell out steps taken and planned to curb proliferation of black money.

There are no clear estimates of the size of India's black economy but the amount is pegged between $462 billion (₹22 lakh crore) and $1.4 trillion (₹77 lakh crore).

Mukherjee will present in Parliament a "White Paper on black money" that draws heavily on the recommendations and findings of the black money committee report drafted by a panel headed by the Central Board of Direct Taxes chairman.

The paper, which is unlikely to name persons suspected to have illegally stowed away money in overseas bank accounts, is expected to propose voluntary disclosure of all high-value transactions.

MONEY FOR NOTHING

No clear estimates of the size of India's black economy

- A BJP task force put the figure between $500bn (₹27.5 lakh crore) and $1.4tn (₹77 lakh crore)
- $500bn, says CBI chief
- $462bn (₹22 lakh crore) stashed away between 1948-2008, estimates Global Financial Integrity
- Govt panel set up to give an estimate. Report in September

Sectors' 'share' in undisclosed income detected in 2011

- 34% Real estate
- 1.8% Medical profession, including hospitals
- 2.4% Educational institutions
- 27% Manufacturing
- 15% Mining
- 19.8% Others

SOURCE: I-T PILOT SURVEY

The committee, set up in May last, has called for stiffer laws to curb generation of black money, including raising to 10 years from seven the maximum jail term for government officials found guilty of accepting bribe.

Setting up of lokpal at the Centre and lokayuktas in states at the earliest for time-bound decisions in graft cases is another suggestion.

Stock brokers and insurance agents may have to provide information as part of a crackdown on money-laundering that impacts the banking and financial sectors. The government is working on changes in the anti-graft law to cover private sector. "While the public sector is over-burdened with archaic rules, the private sector has little or no regulation," an official said, requesting anonymity.

CONTINUED ON PAGE 8

Buying jewellery, property...

CONTINUED FROM PAGE 1

The paper is likely to have a roadmap for a national tax tribunal mandated with sweeping judicial powers to clamp down on illegal transactions — found to be rampant in real estate and construction sectors in a pilot survey by tax authorities. Differences between finance and law ministries have been holding up the proposal for 20 years.

The government plans to turn the screws on 'Ponzi' or multi-level marketing schemes. A central regulator for these get-rich-quick schemes, for which millions of Indians continue to fall, is proposed.

Not only the Opposition and civil society but the Supreme Court, too, has been critical of the government for not doing enough to bring back illicit funds from tax havens.

Hindustan Times
Monday, 21 May 2012

Annexure VII

Hindustan Times
Monday, 28 May 2012

Annexure VIII

According to Gaurav Choudhury & Sanjib Kr. Baruah of Hindustan Times

Black money haze over investments in unlisted firms

Investment in hundreds of unlisted firms are under the government's scanner for funnelling thousands of crores of black money into the legitimate financial system through instruments, which authorities suspect are being used to obscure the source of slush funds.

A pilot survey by the tax authorities reported many instances, particularly in real estate and construction, where companies were borrowing money through "cash" through financial instruments such as "convertible debentures" and "optionally convertible debentures" from scores of investors.

Convertible debentures are instruments through which an investor exchanges the funds that he had lent into equity at a later date, making them legitimate shareholders of the company.

Since these are unlisted companies, the disclosure norms aren't as stringent as these don't come under the Sebi's scanner. There are about 40,000 unlisted companies in India.

The survey showed more than a third of India's black money transactions are believed to be in real estate, including secondary market sales between individuals.

The finance ministry carried out a pilot analysis of tax evasions from data compiled by the I-T department's investigation wing last December.

About a third of this (Rs 1464 crore) was unearthed from real estate, about one-fourth (Rs 1180 crore) from manufacturing sector and about 15% (Rs 645 crore) from the mining sector.

The authorities also suspect many entities to be using "private placement programmes" offered by overseas venture capitalists to introduce dirty money into the legitimate financial system.

High net-worth individuals park money with venture capital funds by depositing money in foreign banks, which are then used to profitably trade in both stock and commodity markets, besides investing in sectors such as real estate by taking advantage of an opaque regulatory architecture.

TRICKS OF THE TRADE

Investment in unlisted private companies
- A person lends ₹10 cr in cash to real-estate firm through convertible debenture
- Firm uses the money to pay vendors for ongoing projects
- Person converts ₹10 cr into equity shares, becomes legitimate shareholder of the firm

Under-invoicing
- A firm buys goods for ₹1 lakh
- Vendor issues bills or invoice on ₹60,000 and receives the balance in cash, keeping it outside the tax net

Property deals
- A plot is sold at ₹20 crore. Buyer pays 50% in cash, rest in cheque
- Seller puts cheque in dormant bank account as property sale proceeds. Part taken out as cash, bank asked for demand draft of huge amount

Hindustan Times
Sunday, 4 March 2012

Annexure IX

According to Shruti Srivastava

India in talks with Switzerland to bring home tax on undeclared money

Shruti Srivastava : New Delhi, Mon Mar 05 2012, 00:15 hrs

After sealing a double taxation avoidance pact with Switzerland, India is now negotiating with the Alpine nation for an arrangement to obtain tax on undeclared money parked in Swiss banks. Under the agreement, the identity of the citizens would not be disclosed.

However, the arrangement is likely to be different from the one entered into by Switzerland with the UK and Germany.

Switzerland had earlier drawn up treaties with Germany and the UK that entails turning in tax from undeclared assets which the citizens of the nations keep in its secretive banks. In fact, Greece was also reportedly working on a similar arrangement with Switzerland.

India is also keen to seal a similar deal but with different terms and conditions. As per the current contours of the agreement, tax is collected by Switzerland on the interest earned by citizens on the deposits. In return, Switzerland asks for market access for its financial institutions and a resolution of the problem of purchasing illegally acquired tax data.

However, given the fact that the interest paid by Swiss banks is very low, the amount generated in form of tax is inconsequential. The average interest rate in Switzerland, decided by the Swiss National Bank, was 1.52 per cent from 2000 until 2010.

India, therefore, wants that the tax collected by Switzerland should be on the deposits and not just the interest earned. Further, India can't provide greater access as demanded because it is already in negotiations with the European Union for a free trade agreement and till its conclusion, any such decision is unlikely to be taken.

"Where is the point in accepting the terms of agreement as they stand? We won't get substantial tax while the names of the clients will also not be revealed. We stand to lose. So we are in negotiation with them. We want that they should either tell us the names or tax the principle amount and not identify the clients," official sources told The Indian Express.

India is also trying for automatic exchange of information with the country, a move Switzerland has so far resisted. Automatic exchange is voluntary but India has been pushing for other countries to join hands in its crusade against black money. It has been advocating the automatic exchange of information for tax purposes and currently has such an arrangement with 10 countries including France, and Germany.

So far, Swiss authorities have said that the final withholding tax is preferable to them than the automatic exchange of bank data.

Recently, Switzerland came out with a statement regarding its initiative to dispel the image of a tax haven. While it emphasised on better due diligence by banks it also said that banks will have to ensure that clients depositing money with Swiss banks will have to declare that they paid taxes in their country of domicile.

The Indian Express
Monday, 5 March 2012

Annexure X

According to Minhaz Merchant article in Times of India the black money is subverting Indian politics. The author is chairman of media group

29 April 2012, 01:06 AM IST

How much does it cost to run a political party? If you go by the audited balance sheet of the Congress for 2009-10 (the latest available), the answer is Rs 525.97 crore. This is a party with several million workers, offices in every one of our 35 states and union territories (UTs) and which fights an average of seven assembly elections each year. The audited balance sheet of India's second largest party, the BJP, is equally modest. Its annual expenditure for 2009-10: Rs 261.74 crore.

In the five recent state assembly elections, the Congress and the BJP together fielded over one thousand candidates. According to the Election Commission's unofficial estimates, the average campaign expenditure of a candidate is between Rs 2.5 crore and Rs 5 crore for an assembly constituency (official EC cap: Rs 25 lakh) and between Rs 5 and Rs 20 crore for a Lok Sabha constituency (official EC cap: Rs 40 lakh).

Take the lower end of the EC's estimate of Rs 2.50 crore per Vidhan Sabha candidate. The thousand-plus Congress and BJP candidates thus spent an estimated Rs 2,500 crore in the space of two months during the five assembly elections earlier this year. The money spent by smaller parties – the BSP, SP and SAD – would take the cash that washed through the electoral system between January and March 2012 to more than Rs 4,000 crore. Add organisational and logistical expenses and the total annual cost of running a political party like the Congress or the BJP would be well over Rs 5,000 crore each — ten times the declared expenditure in their audited balance sheets.

Who pays the difference? The parallel black economy. Estimates vary but the black (cash) economy constitutes roughly a third of India's nominal GDP of Rs 89 lakh crore ($1.78 trillion). That amounts to Rs 30 lakh crore ($600 billion). Of this, around Rs 30,000 crore courses through the political ecosystem every year. The bulk goes to political parties, MPs, MLAs and myriad office-bearers to run their political organisations, fight elections and buy votes. This is quite apart from the money siphoned off in the PDS, MNREGA, Bharat Nirman, public-private-partnership (PPP) projects and civic works and through outright scams like 2G spectrum and the Commonwealth Games.

Political parties are tax-exempt. They pay absolutely no tax – no income tax, no service tax, no professional tax, no TDS. Approximately 3.50 crore Indians do pay income tax. The salaried middle class is the most diligent tax-payer. TDS is extracted from employees every quarter. The proposed move to GST will tax people at the point of consumption, not income. The richer you are, the more you consume — and the more you are taxed. It is a fairer system than one in which the very rich end up paying an average of 10-12% of their gross income as tax and limited companies pay an average of just 13-15% because of generous exemptions and "tax foregone". (In contrast, the defence budget, at 2% of GDP, is less than half of tax foregone on account of exemptions – Rs 5.12 lakh crore in 2010-11 alone.)

A lot of the black money which evades tax washes up at the doorstep of political parties. The resultant quid pro quo between politicians, business and middlemen lies at the root of land, mining and natural resource scams in India. With better political governance, India's economy has the potential to grow at 10% a year. Misgovernance costs the economy at least 2-3% in annual GDP growth on account of corrupt practices, poor infrastructure and retrograde taxation laws.

The long-term remedy for a malignant political ecosystem which rewards scamsters and punishes honest taxpayers is voter education. We need to rapidly achieve a critical threshold of an educated and enlightened electorate. Political parties will find it increasingly difficult to exploit an empowered electorate on spurious grounds of religion, caste and region. Election funding, meanwhile, must be made open and transparent. The Tata and Aditya Birla groups have dedicated trusts to donate funds officially to political parties, a model other corporate houses should follow.

In a reflection of how warped our electoral and political systems have become, the cumulative wealth of India's 10 richest people is 6% ($114.50 billion) of India's GDP. In comparison, the cumulative wealth of America's 10 richest people is a mere 2% ($311.30 billion) of America's GDP. For a poor country where poverty lines are defined at $0.56 a day, there could be no greater indictment of how the black economy has subverted political governance.

The writer is an author and chairman of a media group

The Times of India
Sunday, 29 April 2012

Annexure XI

According to a Economic Times report

Government to get black money estimates by September end

India may be able to get some idea of black money floating its its economy by end September. "The government does not have an estimate of quantum of black money existing in the country. However, based on the recommendations of the Standing Committee on the Finance, the government has commissioned a study by three national-level institutes," minister of state for finance S S Palanimanickam said in a written reply to the Lok Sabha.

These three institutes -- National Institute of Public Finance and Policy, National Institute of Financial Management, National Council for Applied Economic Research -- have been asked to estimate the quantum of unaccounted income or wealth inside and outside the country and its ramifications on national security, he said.

"The study is expected to be completed by September, 2012," he added.

Finance minister Pranab Mukherjee has already indicated that the government will bring out a white paper on black money this session.

Since April, 2009 the Income Tax department has seized undisclosed assets worth Rs 2,644.08 crore domestically, Palanimanickam said.

However, unaccounted income detected in the period was over Rs 45,000 crore through invasive actions. The assets seized are adjusted against the tax demand raised consequent to finalisation of the assessment proceedings, he said.

He said whenever credible information about connivance or involvement of officers or agencies in generation of black money is noticed, it is communicated to the relevant authorities to take appropriate action in accordance with the law.

In another reply, Palanimanickam said recovery of outstanding arrears is an on going process.

So far as recovery of outstanding arrears pertaining to direct taxes is concerned, he said, the dues of Rs 1 crore and above are regularly monitored at a senior level in the Income Tax Department through the mechanism of dossiers to ensure expeditious recovery.

The I-T department recovered Rs 21,791 crore tax arrear during 2011-12 while it was Rs 7,583.90 crore in case of indirect taxes as per the provisional data, he said.

The Economic Times
Sunday, 12 May 2012

Annexure XII

According to Ritu Sarin of Indian Express

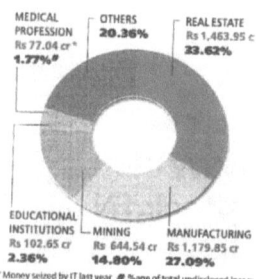

Real estate, mining best to hide income

RITU SARIN
NEW DELHI, MARCH 25

REAL estate, manufacturing, mining, health, education account for over three-quarters of the undisclosed income mopped up by Income Tax authorities last year.

An estimated Rs 3,465 crore of undisclosed income was tracked down in these five sectors according to the minutes of a meeting last month of the Economic Intelligence Council.

Real estate topped the list, accounting for more than a third of the detected undisclosed income, followed by 27.09 per cent in the manufacturing sector. While Rs 1,463 crore was seized from real estate companies, Rs 1,179 crore was garnered from the manufacturing sector.

Besides, Rs 644 crore was collected from the mining sector, Rs 102 crore from educational institutions and Rs 77 crore from the medical sector.

The modus operandi used were "unaccounted cash transactions; manipulation of records; understating receipts; inflating expenses; layering of transactions; and use of specialised software".

Incidentally, the draft report on black money had also identified real estate as "largest part of black money economy", "generating" as well as "consuming" it.

The Economic Times
Saturday, 12 May 2012

Annexure XIII

Dirty money trials to be fast-tracked

Nagendar Sharma & Gaurav Choudhury
■ letters@hindustantimes.com

NEW DELHI: Faced with a thriving black economy that continues to hoodwink authorities by obscuring the source of funds, the government is set to clamp down on the use of dirty money to fund terrorism, arms smuggling, narcotic trade, human trafficking and trading of animal parts.

The finance and law ministries have fine-tuned amendments to the Prevention of Money Laundering Act (PMLA), which will allow officials to investigate the source of unexplained money and frame charges simultaneously with and irrespective of the nature of other crimes allegedly committed.

This follows almost a negligible conviction rate in money-laundering cases – just one since PMLA was enacted in 2002.

Under current laws, PMLA specifies that money-laundering offences be tried only by a special court.

Until now, a person charged with multiple offences, including money-laundering, would be tried for the other crimes first in a different court. The money-laundering probe remained stuck until the other trials were over.

CONTINUED ON PAGE 6

DIRTY MONEY TRIALS TO BE FAST-TRACKED

CONTINUED FROM PAGE 1

"It's for these reasons and the judicial process of trial that the conviction rate in money-laundering offences has remained almost nil," a government source, not willing to be named, told HT.

The rising incidence of alleged money laundering, including in high profile cases such as the 2G spectrum and Commonwealth Games scam, forced the government to introduce amendments that would speed up the probe and conviction.

The government's worry was compounded following a public spat between its top investigating agencies – Central Bureau of Investigation (CBI) and Enforcement Directorate (ED) – in the three-year-old Satyam case, the biggest fraud in India's corporate history.

Serious differences came up between the CBI and ED on which court was competent to try the case where promoters confessed to fudging the company's accounts for several years.

ED, which tracks overseas transactions and money-laundering deals, has pointed out that many such cases of doubtful transactions, some of them suspected to be for funding terror, are stuck for similar reasons.

Hindustan Times
Thursday, 16 August 2012

Annexure XIV

KOZHIKODE: Move over gold, gadgets, and gizmos. Fuelled by increased demand in north India, foreign cigarettes have become the latest lucrative contraband among smugglers.

Customs officials at Karipur International Airport did not have to think twice before subjecting the oversized baggage of Kunjammu Abdul Aziz, a passenger from Dubai, to a detailed search when he landed at the airport last Wednesday.

The search yielded 26,000 foreign cigarettes. The face of Abdul Aziz was still fresh in the minds of customs officials as it was just five months back he was booked for trying to sneak in 32,600 illegal cigarettes.

"Over 60 cases were registered last year in the Karipur Airport against people trying to sneak in commercial quantities of foreign cigarettes. Seven cases have been registered in the first three months this year" said Joannes George, assistant commissioner of customs at the airport.

The favourite brand with the smugglers has been the Gudang Garam, the aromatic flavoured cigarettes made in Indonesia. The brand constitutes around 80% of the illegal cigarettes smuggled through the airport with foreign brands like 555 and Malboro making up the rest.

The clove, mint, and cardamom flavoured sticks commands a premium in Mumbai and north Indian markets, especially in the cold season. Many smokers believe its spice flavour would keep them warm and serve as a defence against cold and fever!

Industry sources says a carton of Gudang Garam could fetch Rs 1,300 in north India during peak winter season, while it would cost below Rs 500 when sourced from free ports like Dubai.

The cigarettes are illegally imported as personal baggage, or via illegal door-to-door courier services mostly from Dubai and other UAE cities.

Directorate of Revenue Intelligence (DRI) officials said that cigarette smuggling has become sophisticated with major organized rackets leading the operations.

"They employ paid carriers who make frequent return trips to UAE staying there for just 2-3 days. Many agents had even acquired frequent flier status with a leading airlines," a DRI official said.

The officials fear that cigarette smuggling could eventually turn into organized crime rackets and force the carriers to smuggle high value goods and narcotics. "There are cases in which the carriers have tried to smuggle saffron concealed in cigarette cartons," a DRI official said.

Meanwhile, law enforcement authorities say the existing customs law does not allow the arrest of the offender as the value of smuggled goods is less than Rs 5 lakh. Customs can only fine them and confiscate the goods.

Usually the offenders are booked for economic offence under section 111 of the Customs Act for illegal imports of goods in commercial quantity.

They are also booked under the Cigarettes and Other Tobacco Products (Packaging and Labelling) Rules, 2006, for trying to distribute cigarette packs without mandatory health warning.

Udayan Lall, director of New Delhi-based Tobacco Institute of India (TII) said high taxes on cigarettes in India have increased the demand for smuggled international brands, which are cheaper. "The large and porous borders of India contribute to the easy availability of smuggled brands," he said.

To stem the influx of contraband, Lall says, the government should ban sale of cigarettes in duty-free shops and exclude it from the list of duty-free baggage. Quoting the figures from Euromonitor International, an international research organization, Lall said illegal cigarettes in India account for 16% of the industry, having grown by 58% between 2004 and 2009 making India the 6th largest illicit cigarette market in the world.

The Times of India
3 April 2012
K. R. Rajeev

Annexure XV

Philip Morris exit seen as blow to Pakistan economy
Khalid Mustafa
Saturday, March 10, 2012

ISLAMABAD: Philip Morris Pakistan, one of the multinationals that contribute billions of rupees to tax revenue annually, has decided to close its Mandara production facility, The News has learnt.

Philip Morris Pakistan (PMP) spokesman when contacted confirmed saying, the heavy tax burden and high cost has led to its decision to close the factory.

The PMP spokesman said the lower purchasing power of the consumer also contributed to the decision to close its plant.

A commerce ministry official remarked that with high taxes, it was not possible for PMP to compete with brands, which evade taxes, are far cheaper, make mockery of pictorial health warning laws, are more affordable, and attractive.

The tax-evading cigarette makers sell more than 14 billion cigarettes in Pakistan every year but are also expanding their production facilities, he said.

Given the enforcement regime in Pakistan where cheap, non-complaint packs are available; it is obvious that operating a compliant business becomes difficult, he said.

Sources in FBR claim that the sale of tax-evaded cigarettes is causing annual loss of more than Rs11 billion to the national exchequer.

It may be recalled here that unable to cope with the higher cost of production and a non level playing field created by the ever increasing availability of low priced tax evaded cigarettes, Philip Morris Pakistan had to announce shutting down its Mandra facility near Rawalpindi.

The Company attributed the decision to high taxation and low consumer affordability and described it as difficult, but necessary.

The details available with this correspondent make a poignant reading. In 2011, the sale of smuggled cigarettes increased by 65 percent, going from 1.0 billion to more than 1.6 billion.

The illicit trade increased by 15 percent going from 18 percent to 21 percent. Nearly 14 billion illicit cigarettes were sold in the country in 2011, out of which over 12 billion cigarettes were local duty evaded. The main cause of this alarming increase in size of illicit cigarettes is the high tax incidence that is currently in place, which in key segments goes up to 81 percent of price of each pack.

As taxes increase, the tax evaders get a competitive advantage and rejoice as their cheap tax-evaded easily available brands become more affordable and attractive to consumers. This tax burden puts the tax complaint business at risk of closure.

According to the market sources, tax evasion has reached such a rampant level that cigarette packs are being openly advertised for sale at as low a price as Rs15, whereas under Federal Excise Law, the minimum selling price for a pack of cigarettes is much more than that.

Experts who understand taxation matters agree such blatant advertisement and subsequent sale of cigarette packs at below the minimum price is clear proof of tax evasion.

Experts believe subjecting legitimate cigarette makers to a higher tax regime will not reduce tobacco consumption in the country as those manufacturers who have historically evaded taxes continue to increase their sales through cheap tax evaded cigarettes. This will only continue to shift supply from tax complaint to tax evaded cheap alternative.

Besides the two large multinational manufacturers, a large number of small scale cigarette makers operate in KPK, Punjab and Azad Kashmir. Many of these brands do not carry pictorial health warning that is mandatory under the existing laws.

There are reliable reports that new cigarette manufacturing units are coming up and expansion in base of these tax evaded products is underway, plants are planned, as the state's ability to check excise duty evasion erodes.

This will put in jeopardy more than US$ 750million, revenue that is contributed by the tax-compliant cigarette industry every year to national exchequer.

The end of duty evaded cigarettes will reduce access of cheap cigarettes for the youth. The youth starts smoking through low priced cigarettes and one sure way to protect the future generations from the curse of smoking is to implement the taxation and the regulatory regime and ensure that menace of cheap brands is wiped away.

The News
Saturday 10 March 2012

Annexure XVI

Contraband cigarettes market estimated at Rs 1,900 crore this year

PTI Jan 15, 2012, 04.29PM IST

NEW DELHI: High excise duty on cigarettes in India has resulted in the growth of contraband trade of the product with the total market estimated to reach Rs 1,900 crore this year, up nearly 12 per cent from the previous year, according to industry estimates.

In 2010-11, the size of contraband cigarettes market in India was around Rs 1,700 crore.

According to industry players, 17 billion cigarette sticks are smuggled into the country every year, making India the sixth highest consumer of smuggled cigarettes in the world.

Experts cited the huge price differential in India and neighbouring countries as one of the primary reasons for the increase in smuggling of cigarette in India.

Low cost cigarettes make their way to India from countries like China, Myanmar, Nepal, Bangladesh, Indonesia and Pakistan, they said.

"Smuggled and contraband cigarettes are becoming a bigger and bigger problem in India. There are lot of illegal cigarettes, which are smuggled from outside India and even counterfeit products are also sold in huge quantity," an official working with a cigarettes company said.

The government needs to take serious action to control the illegal trade, he added.

The smuggled cigarettes of 80 mm size could still be cheaper than an authentic regular sized 70 mm filter cigarette in India. "This is a direct threat to the filter segment which constitutes 69 per cent of the total Indian cigarette market," the official said.

When asked about the factors behind the increase in illegal trade of the product, he said, "Extreme high excise duty and VAT rate on cigarettes in India make smuggling a particularly attractive proportion."

Citing an example, he said the total tax on a legitimate Rs 100 pack is as high as Rs 68, but as contraband cigarettes do not pay any of those taxes, they are priced at up to Rs 80 and still allow a high margin.

According to the industry estimates, 60 million sticks are smuggled every month in Mumbai followed by 35 million sticks in Delhi and 20 million sticks per month in Pune, Bangalore and Hyderabad.

The Economic Times
15 January 2012

Annexure XVII

Contraband cigarettes market estimated at Rs 1,900 cr this year

High excise duty on cigarettes in India has resulted in the growth of contraband trade of the product with the total market estimated to reach Rs 1,900 crore this year, up nearly 12 per cent from the previous year, according to industry estimates.

In 2010-11, the size of contraband cigarettes market in India was around Rs 1,700 crore.

According to industry players, 17 billion cigarette sticks are smuggled into the country every year, making India the sixth highest consumer of smuggled cigarettes in the world.

Experts cited the huge price differential in India and neighbouring countries as one of the primary reasons for the increase in smuggling of cigarette in India.

Low cost cigarettes make their way to India from countries like China, Myanmar, Nepal, Bangladesh, Indonesia and Pakistan, they said.

"Smuggled and contraband cigarettes are becoming a bigger and bigger problem in India. There are lot of illegal cigarettes, which are smuggled from outside India and even counterfeit products are also sold in huge quantity," an official working with a cigarettes company said.

The government needs to take serious action to control the illegal trade, he added.

The smuggled cigarettes of 80 mm size could still be cheaper than an authentic regular sized 70 mm filter cigarette in India. "This is a direct threat to the filter segment which constitutes 69 per cent of the total Indian cigarette market," the official said.

When asked about the factors behind the increase in illegal trade of the product, he said, "Extreme high excise duty and VAT rate on cigarettes in India make smuggling a particularly attractive proportion."

Citing an example, he said the total tax on a legitimate Rs 100 pack is as high as Rs 68, but as contraband cigarettes do not pay any of those taxes, they are priced at up to Rs 80 and still allow a high margin.

According to the industry estimates, 60 million sticks are smuggled every month in Mumbai followed by 35 million sticks in Delhi and 20 million sticks per month in Pune, Bangalore and Hyderabad.

The Hindu
15 January 2012

Annexure XVIII

Tobacco tax offers smuggler incentive

SAMBIT SAHA

Calcutta, Sept. 1: The Bengal government today raised the value-added tax (VAT) on cigarettes to 20 per cent from 13.5 per cent, desisting from hitting the 30 per cent ceiling permissible after a switch earlier this week.

The tax increase is unlikely to change the price many consumers pay as it will be largely borne by cigarette manufacturers and wholesalers. But the increased levy runs the risk of creating an "arbitrage opportunity" that can encourage smuggling from other states and somewhat blunt the government's drive to generate more revenue.

While presenting the Finance Bill on Monday, finance minister Amit Mitra had said tobacco products were being put in a schedule that allowed VAT up to 30 per cent. The new rate, which was not specified then, was notified by the finance department today.

What smokers pay for a pack of the most popular brands is expected to remain untouched since maximum retail prices are unlikely to be changed. ITC, which manufactures three out of every four packs sold in the country, sells all its popular brands at the same rate across the country, although the VAT rates differ from state to state.

However, other players like Godfrey Phillips are likely to raise the prices of their low-priced brands at the retail level as well.

In either case, the VAT increase in Bengal opens up a window of lucrative opportunity for unscrupulous operators if they smuggle in cigarette cartons from other states where the same tax is lower.

For instance, just one carton of Gold Flake Kings can make a smuggler richer by as much as Rs 68 if it is brought in from neighbouring Orissa **(see chart)**. A carton is not much bigger than a loaf of bread and a huge quantity can easily be smuggled in after hoodwinking law-enforcers.

The smugglers' margin may come down a bit if cigarette manufacturers do not pass the entire burden to the trade.

The tax on tobacco products is 13.5 per cent in Orissa and Bihar and 14 per cent in Jharkhand — all below the new slab of 20 per cent notified by Bengal today.

This means that a stretch of "tobacco tax haven" will run alongside Bengal, unwittingly tempting traders to link up with smuggling channels, make a killing and deny revenue to the cash-strapped coffers of the state.

The problem could be more acute in districts that border other states. "Unless the administration keeps a close vigil, smuggling would impact revenue collection on account of cigarettes," an industry executive said.

Tobacco manufacturers ITC and Godfrey Phillips declined to comment. Udayan Lall, the director of Tobacco Institute of India, said: "We always request moderation on taxes. Ultimately, they prove to be counterproductive."

An industry veteran raised another area of concern: sale of contraband cigarettes. "High and differential tax rates provide an attractive arbitrage opportunity for smuggling, tax evasion and incentive for illegal manufacturing of stocks," he pointed out.

It is unlikely that the entire burden will be passed on to the retailer by the wholesaler and the manufacturer. Industry observers said manufacturers like ITC might take a hit on their profitability and try to cushion a part of the impact on the wholesalers. But some of the increase is expected to be passed on to the trade channel (wholesalers and shops)

The Telegraph

Annexure XIX

NEW DELHI, MAY 17, 2012: As per Ministry of Home, 24 persons have been arrested and **Rs. 71.45 crore worth smuggled goods** were seized on Indo-Bangladesh border in 2011-12. The **contraband smuggled includes** Fake Indian Currency Notes, readymade garments, food grains, cattle, **cigarettes** and medicines, narcotics (including phensedyl syrup). This was stated by Mr Mullappally Ramachandran, Minister of State of Home Affairs, in written reply in the Rajya Sabha yesterday.

The Government has adopted a multi-pronged approach for effective domination and to check illegal activities including infiltration on Indo-Bangladesh border. The steps taken in this regard inter-alia includes:

++ Effective domination of the border by carrying out round the clock surveillance of the borders by patrolling nakas (border ambushes) and by deploying observation posts all along the International Border. Riverine segments of IB are being patrolled and dominated with the help of water crafts/speed boats/floating Border Out Posts (BOPs) of BSF water wings.

++ Construction of fencing, patrol roads, floodlighting and additional Border Out Posts.

++ Induction of force multipliers and Hi-Tech surveillance. Constant efforts are being made to procure the latest surveillance equipments for further enhancing the border domination.

++ Up-gradation of intelligence network and co-ordination with sister agencies. Conduct of special operations along with border.

There are reports of Bangladeshi nationals having entered into India without valid travel documents. As entry of such Bangladeshi nationals into the country is clandestine and surreptitious, it is not possible to have a correct estimate of such illegal immigrants living in different states in the country, he said.

Annexure XX

Cheap branded cigarettes are more lethal

Its in fact the nicotine and tobacco in cheap cigarettes which are more harmful compared to the branded ones, where there are careful measures taken to keep it as less harmful as possible

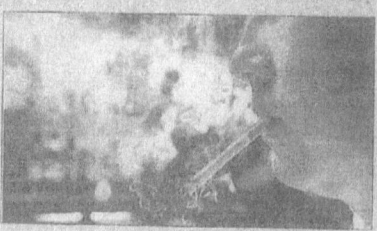

■ **Business Reporter**

CIGARETTE Smoking and chewing tobacco flavoured gutkha amongst school going teenagers has become a common trend. Around educational institutions like schools, colleges and coaching centres the pan kiosks can be seen decorated with colourful packaged flavoured tobacco pouches and shelves full of cigarette packets.

In this whole business not only tobacco companies are enjoying handsome sales but the kiosks owners are making money while ignoring the health of future citizens.

The situation turns more touching when school and college going children start smoking cheaper cigarettes. As smoking cigarette is injurious to health, but is even more poison when cheap unbranded cigarettes are used.

Experts warn that while the big companies keep a watch over the quality through stringent methods, the companies selling filter cigarettes use sub standard tobacco and other raw materials like cigarette paper and plastic fibber filter. Excess use of such cigarettes can even lead to poisoning of the lungs, leading to death of the user.

Even after relentless campaign against cigarette smoking in public places, the market of cheaper cigarettes is increasing fastly. The substandard raw material being used in cheap tobacco products may open a new health threat as the smoker puffs nicotine goes in deep with inhale, while smoking the cheaper cigarette is the real damage causing activity.

As the flavour part of cheap cigarette pipes is intense, people normally ignores the quality of material used in it and do not think about their lungs health. These cheap filter cigarettes have poor quality nitrate paper.

Nicotine being a highly addictive material is found in high range of cheaper cigarettes. The small amount of nicotine creates a pleasant feeling which makes the smoker want to smoke more, and cheap quality material makes its intense and more harmful. Excess of nicotine and other harmful material in cigarettes also affects the chemistry of the brain and central nervous system.

Dr Nisha Baghel, a consultant informed that "Nicotine is not only a harmful component in cigarettes there is a whole array of harmful component present. Cigarette smoke is a complex mixture of compounds. Besides usual stimulant nicotine, cigarette smoke contains tar, which is made up of more than 4000 chemicals including around 60 known carcinogenic chemicals".

The administration should initiate proper check over the sale of tobacco containing pan masala, gutkha and quality of cigarette and other such products.

The Hitavada
Sunday, 18 March 2012

Annexure XXI

Annexure XXII

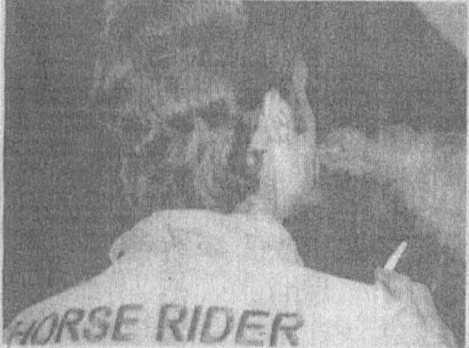

The Times of India

Annexure XXIII

Illegal trading of tobacco mushrooming in State

By Kirit Joshi
RAIPUR, Dec 5

NATIONALLY admired as the most emerging state in the country, Chhattisgarh is not far behind its counterparts as far as flourishing of tobacco products manufactured/ imported illegally in the State. Ironically, the illegal trading of tobacco products, cigarette in particular, is mushrooming under the very nose of authorities concerned in the government. In a startling revelation, more than 8 million cigarette sticks are sold annually in the State which is around 9-10 per cent of the tax-evading cigarettes.

In context of Chhattisgarh, State Government has imposed 14 per cent VAT (Value Added Tax) on branded cigarettes apart 7.5 per cent entry tax as all branded cigarettes are manufactured in other states and supplied to Chhattisgarh.

In this way, the local consolidated taxes on cigarette pile up to 21.5 per cent in the state. In the perspective of local or tax evading cigarettes, a manufacturer earns a profit up to 21.5 per cent on the rate along with the additional income comes from the finish products supplied to retailers.

However, these categories of cigarette manufacturers have the option to supply their products at cheaper rate and increase the profit margin

of retailers. A section of the customers opt for cheaper puff resulting in heavy loss of revenue collection in government exchequer.

Apart from readily available local tendu leaves, the alarmingly increasing in number of retailers and customers have nourished the chain of manufacturer-customer thereby increasing the market share of tax-evading cigarette to around 10 per cent. The business is flourishing in open violation of norms.

Being a strategic location, ready availability of raw materials and harsh tax structure, Chhattisgarh has provided the stability to illegal cigarette business. Escaping the clutches of State Tax Department with the

"Complicated tax structure at national and state level has forced the legitimate cigarette traders to increase the cost of each stick. Taking advantage of the galloping prices, different size of locally made filter cigarettes are available between Rs 1 to Rs 2.00 each stick. Customers have adjusted to the flavour of locally manufactured products compromising on health hazards instead of going for branded regular filter cigarette range starting from Rs 3.00 each stick, opened a few traders"

deftly managed business policy or the most happening issue that raked the nation shadowing all italics from A to Z except 'C' (corruption) dominating all circles and sections on the society.

The tax evading retailers have better profit margin against invested amount while customers cited low cost of locally manufactured cigarette in comparison to branded ones that promoted for development of tax-evading cigarette market. Harsh taxation on cigarettes at the national level has resulted in generation of over 75 per cent of the total tax collected from tobacco trading sector. However, in terms of consumption it accounts to only 15 - 20 per cent of the total tobacco consumption at the national level.

Talking to The Hitavada, Sales

tax Commissioner Ganesh Shankar Mishra said he had not information relating to locally manufactured tax-evading cigarettes available in the market. He further added that if any information is received on the issue, stern action will be taken against the illegal manufacturers and traders.

On being brought to the knowledge, District Collector Dr. Rohit Yadav informed that he was unaware of any highly toxic locally manufactured cigarettes being sold in the capital and no such complaint was brought to his knowledge.

If quality is concerned, State Food and Adulteration Department should initiate action against sellers of the highly toxic cigarettes. However, he assured of necessary measures to check the sale toxic cigarettes manufactured locally and sold in Raipur

The Hitavada

Annexure XXIV

Traders get past Rajasthan smoke barrier, a third of tobacco smuggled

APEKSHA JAMPURKAR SHETTI

AN EFFORT by the Rajasthan government to curb tobacco addiction in the state by doubling Value Added Tax (VAT) on tobacco products seems to have gone up in smoke. In an indication of the blackmarket rampant in tobacco in the state, in just two operations recently, the Commercial Taxes Department has recovered dues to Rs 1 crore in taxes and penalties from traders, while around hundred cases are presently under investigation.

"We received information that tobacco products were being transported from neighbouring states where VAT is lower. In April we recovered Rs 49 lakh from 96 centres and in June Rs 47 lakh from 81 centres," Commercial Taxes Deputy Commissioner (Anti-Evasion) and spokesperson Omni Ram said.

While VAT on tobacco products is 40 per cent in Rajasthan, probably the highest in India, it is 6 per cent in states like Haryana, Madhya Pradesh and Punjab, it is around 20 per cent.

According to records with the Commercial Taxes Department, highest recoveries have been made in Ajmer, Alwar, Banswara and Pali districts of Rajasthan.

Tobacco wholesalers say the blackmarket trade is the only way they can now turn a profit. A wholesaler from Jaipur admits they have been getting in products from neighbouring states since April this year, saying this makes up "at least one-third of the supply".

At the Rajasthan Police put this out, transporting tobacco products is easier as compared to alcohol. According to a senior official, tobacco products are usually stored in a godown just across the border from Rajasthan and transported at night.

"In this illicit trade, a truck enters Rajasthan carrying goods worth Rs 8 to 10 lakh but the product is distributed before entering an urban centre. Smaller couriers then transport individual boxes to traders," he said.

According to Ram, the first raids were conducted in April. "In the operation that concluded on April 7, we covered 96 centres, including 48 cities, out of which we booked 45 cases and recovered Rs 49 lakh. In the same operation, 57 cases are presently under investigation," said the Deputy Commissioner.

In the second operation that concluded on June 21, covering 81 centres including 59 cities, the department booked 44 cases, recovering Rs 47 lakh, while another 37 are under investigation.

PAGE 1 ANCHOR

State had hiked VAT on tobacco products to 40%, among highest in the country

The Indian Express

Annexure XXV

Traders get past Rajasthan smoke barrier, a third of tobacco smuggled

APURVA
JAIPUR, AUGUST 1

AN EFFORT by the Rajasthan government to curb tobacco addiction in the state by doubling Value Added Tax (VAT) on tobacco products seems to have gone up in smoke. In an indication of the blackmarket rampant in tobacco in the state, in just two operations recently, the Commercial Taxes Department has recovered close to Rs 1 crore in taxes and penalties from traders, while around hundred cases are presently under investigation.

"We received information that tobacco products were being transported from neighbouring states where VAT is lower. In April we recovered Rs 49 lakh from 96 centres and in June Rs 47 lakh from 81 centres," Commercial Taxes Deputy Commissioner (Anti-Evasion) Gyana Ram said.

While VAT on tobacco products is 40 per cent in Rajasthan, probably the highest in India, in neighbouring states like Haryana, Madhya Pradesh and Punjab, it is around 20 per cent.

According to records with the Commercial Taxes Department, highest recoveries have been made in Ajmer, Alway, Bharatpur and Pali districts of Rajasthan.

Tobacco wholesalers say the blackmarket trade is the only way they can now turn a profit. A wholesaler from Jaipur admits they have been getting in products from neighbouring states since April this year, saying this makes up "at least one-third of the supply".

As the Rajasthan Police points out, transporting tobacco products is easier as compared to alcohol. According to a senior official, tobacco products are usually stored in a godown just across the border from Rajasthan and transported at night.

"In this illicit trade, a truck enters Rajasthan carrying goods worth Rs 8 to 10 lakh but the product is distributed before entering an urban centre. Smaller couriers then transport individual boxes to traders," he said.

According to Ram, the first raids were conducted in April. "In the operation that concluded on April 7, we covered 96 centres, including 48 cities, out of which we booked 45 cases and recovered Rs 49 lakh. In the same operation, 57 cases are presently under investigation," said the Deputy Commissioner.

In the second operation that concluded on June 21, covering 81 centres including 50 cities, the department booked 44 cases, recovering Rs 47 lakh, while another 37 are under investigation.

The Indian Express

Annexure XXVI

Hindustan Times

Annexure XXVII

ILLEGAL CIGARETTES TRADE ROBS WEALTH AND HEALTH

The state is also emerging as a hotbed of the illegal cigarettes trade in India as it represents one of the largest markets for this illicit trade in the upper northern region. The locally manufactured tax-evading cigarettes, it is learnt, have a 9% share of the cigarette market in the state.

The harsh taxation on cigarettes in India is the chief cause for the huge and growing market for illegal cigarettes. Despite accounting for a meagre 15% share of total tobacco consumption, cigarettes generate over 75% of the tax revenue from tobacco.

According to the Euromonitor report, Illicit Trade in Tobacco Products, India is the world's sixth largest market for illicit cigarettes. Although the category of 'illicit cigarettes' also includes smuggled international brands, it consists principally of duty-evaded cigarettes manufactured domestically by small, unscrupulous units.

These units do not pay the high excise and VAT levied on cigarettes, and conduct flourishing clandestine businesses.

The manufacture of illegal cigarettes gained tremendous momentum after the Union Budgets of 2008-2009 and 2010-11, when central excise duty rates increased by an unprecedented 42%. Legitimate cigarette manufacturers were forced to vacate the hitherto affordable price points

TAX TALES

In Himachal, the VAT on cigarettes is currently 16% but there is an added local tax of 4% entry tax, which takes the tax up to 20%. There is also an additional carriage tax of Rs 2 per kg up to 250 km and Rs 4 per kg above 250 km. While VAT itself has not risen significantly from 12.5% in 2007, a high entry tax has caused an unfavourable total local sales tax, thereby giving an impetus to the illegal trade

of Rs 1 and Rs 1.50 per stick, and the vacuum was rapidly filled by illegal regular size filter cigarettes that began to be sold to consumers at Re 1 per stick (or Rs 10/- per packet of 10 cigarettes). The illegal cigarettes are thus available to consumers at the price of bidis. The MRP on unregulated packs is Rs 14-21, but they are often sold at Rs 6-10. A large section of consumers finds these prices irresistible, and this has helped certain illegal brands to establish themselves as the 'common man's brand'.

The trade in illegal cigarettes in Himachal and other states in India is growing rapidly. This clearly demonstrates that the discriminatory tax policy against cigarettes does not decrease overall tobacco consumption, and neither does it lead to a higher collection of taxes. It simply catalyses the growth of the illegal cigarettes trade, and compels people to switch to cheaper illegal cigarettes or other cheap tobacco products which are far more harmful than legally manufactured cigarettes.

~ J Y Ghuman

The Times of India

Annexure XXVIII

Annexure XIX

हिमाचल में अवैध सिगरेट का कारोबार

शिमला| हिमाचल में अवैध सिगरेट का कारोबार राज्य के राजस्व को भी नुक्सान पहुंचा रहा है। तंबाकू उद्योग द्वारा करवाए गए अध्ययन के अनुसार हिमाचल में तस्करी कर लाए गए इंटरनेशनल ब्रांड के सिगरेट बड़ी संख्या में बेचे जा रहे हैं, पर कोई एक्साइज या वैट टैक्स नहीं भरा जाता है। पूरे देश को इस कारोबार से दो हजार करोड़ रुपए के राजस्व का नुक्सान होता है जबकि हिमाचल को भी अच्छा खासा राजस्व खोना पड़ रहा है। ऐसे में इस तरफ ध्यान दिए जाने की जरूरत है।

Dainik Bhaskar

Annexure XXX

DLA Media

Annexure XXXI

Annexure XXXII

Observer

Annexure XXXIII

Patrika

Annexure XXXIV

अवैध सिगरेट के लिए उपजाऊ क्षेत्र बना उप्र

अशोक सिंह। वाराणसी

यूरोमॉनीटर रिपोर्ट, इलिसिट ट्रेड इन टोबैको

वैट की अधिकता के कारण हो रही है चोरी

राज्य को प्रतिवर्ष 186 करोड़ का राजस्व घाटा

Pioneer Hindi

Annexure XXXV

टैक्स बढ़ाने से तस्करों की बल्ले-बल्ले

तम्बाकू उत्पाद

कार्यालय संवाददाता @ जयपुर

गुटखा-सिगरेट आदि तम्बाकू उत्पादों पर वैट दुगना करने से राज्य में इन उत्पादों की तस्करी बढ़ गई है। पड़ोसी राज्यों में कम टैक्स के कारण सीमावर्ती इलाकों में बड़ी मात्रा में तस्करी के जरिये ये उत्पाद राजस्थान में लाकर बेचे जा रहे हैं। ऐसे में न सरकार को पूरा टैक्स मिल रहा है, न उपभोक्ता को माल सस्ता मिल रहा है, वहीं ईमानदार छोटे व्यापारी तस्करी की मनमानी के कारण हैरान हैं।

राज्य के पिछले बजट में इन उत्पादों पर सरकार ने वैट 20 से बढ़ा कर 40 फीसदी कर दिया था, जबकि पड़ोसी राज्यों पंजाब, हरियाणा, उत्तर प्रदेश, मध्यप्रदेश, गुजरात व दिल्ली में 20 प्रतिशत के आसपास ही टैक्स लगता है। टैक्स चोरी रोकने के लिए

वैट दर	
पंजाब	20
हरियाणा	20
दिल्ली	20
गुजरात	28
मध्यप्रदेश	26
उत्तर प्रदेश	13

(दर प्रतिशत में)

जिम्मेदार वाणिज्यिक कर विभाग भी स्वीकार करता है कि राज्य में टैक्स ज्यादा होने के कारण तस्करी की समस्या तो है, लेकिन इस साल दो बार अभियान चला कर कार्रवाई करने तथा नियमित नजर रख कर इसमें कमी लाई जा रही है।

छोटे रास्ते बने मुसीबत

पत्रिका नेटवर्क से मिली खबरों के अनुसार अलवर, श्रीगंगानगर, भरतपुर, धौलपुर, सिरोही, जालोर,

कोटा, चित्तौड़गढ़, झालावाड़ जिलों में बसों, मिनी ट्रकों व निजी वाहनों के जरिये छोटे रास्तों से राज्य की सीमा के उस पार से माल आता है। यह वाणिज्यिक कर विभाग की नजर में नहीं आ पाता। विभाग में टैक्स चोरी रोकने के जिम्मेदार अति. आयुक्त ज्ञानाराम खुद बताते हैं कि अभियान चला अप्रेल में 48 शहरों में 96 डीलरों व जून में 50 शहरों में 81 डीलरों पर कार्रवाई की। एक करोड़ कर चोरी पकड़ी गई।

Rajasthan Patrika

Annexure XXXVI

Satana Jagran
22 March 2012

Index

ACMA member companies, awareness program, 95
Anti-counterfeit and anti-smuggling laws, 35-41
   laws, important issues to be addressed in the enforcement of, 38, 39
Anton Piller orders and John Doe orders, 38
Automotive components supply chain, 81, 82
   parts and after market parts, 104

Bandyopadhyay, Orchie, 63
Bettcher, Douglas, 54
Bhushan, Prashant (member of Team Anna), 132
Brand India, 65
Building interoperable services, 24, 25
Bureau of Indian Standards Act (BIS), 126, 127

Chandra, Meenu, 70
Chawan, S.B., 72
Check counterfeiting, need for amending laws, 28-30
China, 59
Chinese impact, 87, 88
Compliance marketing, 127
Component manufacturers and ACMA, 94, 95
Consumer education, 127
   Protection Act 1986, 107
   Right of Access to Non-Hazardous Product, 117-119
Contact Act 1872, 105
Contraband cigarettes big business, 71-74
   in India, 55

Copyright Act 1957, 28, 37, 111
Counterfeit, 35
   spare parts, 47
Counterfeit and smuggling, research report findings, 132, 133
Counterfeited parts, most commonly, 75
Counterfeiting and directive practices, trends in, 16-20
   factors impacting, 83, 84
   its impact on automotive sector, 74-130
   piracy pose danger for consumers, 58-63
   in alcoholic beverages, 57
   in general, 74
   in India, important factors responsible for, 35, 36
   in India, major sectors affected by, 36, 37
   market in India, size of, 89
   of auto parts in India, 76-78, 81
Curbing counterfeiting through taxation, 42-46
Customs Act 1962, 38

Dahiya, Rakesh, 59
Designs Act, 112, 113
Drugs and Cosmetics Act, 120-123
Dumping, 31
Duty unpaid cigarettes, 71, 72

EFPIA (European Federation of Pharmaceutical Industries and Associations), 26-27
Enforcement agencies, 28
Essential of Commodities Act, 1955, 106

EU Directive on General Product Safety, 114-118

FDI, 51
FICCI, 28, 31, 48, 60, 62
    CASCADE and public awareness on counterfeiting and smuggling, 66-68
Food Adulteration Act, 123-125
    and Drug Administration, 59
Fuel consumption and pollution, 92, 93

G20 member countries, 15, 16
Global auto components scenario, 74
Globalization, 61
GSI and ISO technical committee, 24
    India, 13, 14
    MobileCom group, 25-27
Gupta, Naresh, 59

Illegal cigarettes, 68-70
Illicit trade, impact of, 36

Importing, 85
India's auto component imports from China, 89
Indian auto components sector, 78-81
Indian manufacturing industry, challenges facing, 31-35
Industries affected by counterfeiting, 47-57
Industry challenges, 14-16
Information discovery, 22-24
Intellectual Property Rights (Imported Goods) Enforcement Rules, 2007, 116, 117

Jha, P.C., 46
Job losses, 91
Joshi, Yashwardhan, 133

Law Ministry, 29
Legal framework in India, 66
    issues and legislative aspects, 103
    position in India, 37, 38

Loss of Government Tax Revenue, 90

Manufacturing, 84
Measures to be adopted, 40, 41
Misra, Bejon, 55-57
Motor Vehicles Act and Rules, 119
Mukherjee, Pranab, 131
Mumbai Police, 49

Packaging, 84
Patents Act, 110
Public awareness, sword against counterfeiting and smuggling, 64-71

Rajput, Anil, 73
Regulations, 72
Regulatory framework, 49
Respondents, profile of, 101
Road accident deaths, 93
    in India, 91, 92
Sales of Goods Act, 105
Sethi, Rahul, 58, 62
Shortcomings of existing legislations, 86, 87
Spurious medicine, 55
Standards of Weights and Measures Act, 1976, 108, 109
Stop Counterfeiting in Manufactured Goods Act, 125

Tarnishing brand India, 65
Trade Mark Act 1999, 28, 37, 112

UNs, 64
U.S. FDA's efforts, 26
USTR report, 62

VAT, 49, 62
Visibility, 20-22

White Paper on black money, 131-133
WHO, 26, 35, 54, 60
    reports, 15
WIPO Internet Treaties, 62
WTO, 31